The Perfect Appearance

Published by:
Best Global Publishing
PO Box 9366
Brentwood
Essex
CM13 1ZT
United Kingdom

www.bestglobalpublishing.com

In time we
hate that
which we often
fear.

William Shakespeare

Always for Trixie

For Peter Marshall. A Hero. An Inspiration.

Also for my mum and dad for giving me the life I have. I love you both. And Benjay, my bro.

Susie

Red faced, eyes blurred, cheeks flaming, ears ringing, she crawled along the new cream carpet, digging and clawing her fingers into it, trying to muster the strength to get away. Get away from this place. “Get away from him.” she muttered quietly to herself.

The sky had turned dark, and the small, modest house shone underneath the moonlight. The old, oak rocking chair sat silently in the corner, as she pulled herself up using the wooden banister at the top of the stairs. She looked around herself, noticing her Picasso print hanging loosely on one corner, against the newly painted white walls.

Every thing went silent. Her crying had stopped along time ago, his mocking, teasing voice had been muted, and all that could be heard, was a deadly silence.

Her hands trembled violently as she looked at the blurry walls in front of her, trying to clear her mind and think about her next move.

His veins were pumping with the whisky he had guzzled only hours before. A nervous gasp stuck in her throat as she heard movement on the stairs below her. Still trembling and shaking, she peered over the top, looking down into the narrow gap of darkness, like a pathway leading to her endless torment. Her freedom was away away from the monster with whom she was joined in holy matrimony.

“Susssie” the patronising sing song voice came from below the stairs.

She stiffened, not daring herself to make a move or reply. She knew if she did, then he would have her. Forever. Until the end of time.

Susie looked at the stairs leading downwards, she felt herself stiffen as her spine shivered with fear. She felt like a small prey running away from the predator. She could almost see the plan he had set out for her, to chase her, watch her squirm, then just as she was at breaking point, move in for the kill, and so far, Susie had allowed it to happen.

Later, she sat hard against the wall, trembling fiercely, as his eyes stared back at her. Wide, open, never wavering from her own. They didn't blink, they didn't move, just stared back at Susie. She thought back to the day they married; it had never been anything other than an arrangement, she had been forced to marry him, but she had hoped it could turn into something more.
And now he was dead.
Susie blinked. Then looked at her hand, clenching it tightly, and then releasing it.
She studied her fingers, shaking in disbelief at what she'd done. The word echoed in her brain.
She glanced back to Toby, laying there on then kitchen floor, and once again, those open eyes stared back at her. Still mocking her, still laughing at her.
Susie stood up on shaky legs, and steadied herself by holding onto the table. Her breath caught in her throat as those cold blue eyes stared at her, before she turned her back and waked away.
When she walked into the lounge she looked out of the windows, and saw it was snowing like confetti on the devils parade. She sat down silently. She placed her hands in her lap, neatly crossed over one another. The moonlight poured into the darkened room and shone upon her pale face as a small smile rose on her face.

Her eyes strayed over to the bottom of the stairs, where she could see a puddle of Jack Daniel's whisky, as it seeped through the cream carpet, staining it, leaving a painful reminder of his presence.
Suddenly a flare of fury rose within her as she got up and marched towards the stain. Staring down at it, she could still see the blue mocking eyes staring back at her, the same eyes that had watched her beg for mercy when in the past he had threatened to beat her.
She went into the kitchen, past his motionless body, and picked up a tea towel.
As she was scrubbing the stain, all anger vanished, and her eyes started to flood with salty tears of pain. Huge, racking sobs shook her whole body, and as her head fell into her hands and she fell to her side, crying desperately.
Her mind showed her what happened, over and over again. His laughter echoing in her ears and his harsh voice telling her she was nothing. His arm raising for another violent attack on her, and then she, suddenly, looking up into his eyes, and watching how they had betrayed the fear he felt for himself.
Another sob escaped her, as she lay on the floor. All that could be heard from outside the cottage, was distressed animals screaming like desperate pleas for help, and the clock, ticking slowly, signifying each painful second that passed by.
The sound when she stuck him down, vibrated in her ears, she didn't want to think about the deafening, haunting reverberation that had echoed throughout the cottage. She didn't want to think at all. She sat up and looked around herself. Her lips rose in a tiny, self-mocking smile. She then stood up on unsteady legs, and wiped her face clean of tears.

As she walked into the kitchen, she looked at the body still laying where it had been earlier, having not moved an inch. Its motionless limbs were sprawled across the white tiled floor, one arm flung carelessly towards the dented frying pan, as the blood dripped slowly, almost teasingly, from his head.

Her eyes focused on the crimson liquid which had settled on the floor. She saw the path which it had run, in and out of the tiles, around the tiles, onto the tiles, drowning them until no white could be seen, like the devil claiming Susie's soul and all the good she once had inside her. Her eyes focused out of the window and she looked at the stars in the sky and the moon shining brightly. Her hand clench and un-clenched as she thought of what she could do. The dark shadow, that had haunted her since she married him, ceased to exist now, but the burden of knowing how it had been lifted away from her shoulders, was enough for anyone to take. She knew who would help her, and she picked up the telephone and pushed the numbers slowly. What if no one helped her?

Chapter one

I'm stuck. Ha! And where had that thought come from? It wasn't as if Connor didn't relish these few precious moments where he managed to get away from his frosty wife. He sighed, ah it was obvious why he liked these times to himself, it was because he could *be* himself. *Who is the real Connor? A man who likes society to believe he's a respectful human? But what would they do if they knew the real you?* His wife's haunting words drifted through his mind. Those harsh questions, questions he'd asked himself time and time again and still had no answer. "It's 'cos you don't want to know" he mumbled to himself. Since a young child his father had always drummed the importance of appearances, until it had embedded itself to an extent where he wasn't quite sure where his facade left off and the real Connor began. Perhaps everyone lived trying to make others view them as something they weren't. Hell, he wouldn't be surprised if his wife tore off her cool, elegant face and revealed a wolf bearing its teeth, with a ready smile to rip him to pieces. Oh, how it would be easier if it were that simple. At least he would know what to expect if his wife was a wolf, he would make sure he had weapons ready; he'd be ready to defend. But her cool, neutral expression was more dangerous. He wasn't sure if she would undermine him, jab at him, threaten him with his secrets, or if she would show him that rare affection she seemed to have lost all those years ago. God, the last time they'd had sex she'd even wore that neutral face, not giving any hint of pleasure, or disgust. Connor wondered what he would do, if he saw disgust. Of course his male pride would be hurt, that was normal for any self-respecting man who cared about the pleasure of his companion. He mostly believed he would feel elated, at least he would find that she was capable of still *feeling* something, because if she didn't feel then there was no telling what she was capable of. No, Connor shook his head, a small smile forming; of course she still felt emotions. This was his wife, his Caroline. His Caroline who had laughed and played and been so forceful and passionate in their lovemaking, that he fell in love with her fiery, happy nature the moment he saw her. Ah those days seemed so long ago now, the simplicity of waking up, wondering where the day will take you. Now he woke up, knowing what he had to do, knowing how it would go, knowing when he would be home and knowing he would be going to bed alone that night, as he had done for so many years. The only part of his day he enjoyed was right now, this moment, as he sat with his whiskey in his glass, the welcoming silence of his house, and the darkness soothing his troubling thoughts. He liked sitting in the dark, behind his oak desk, with the continuing mountain of papers, which, even if he worked all day, would creep higher and higher.

There aren't enough hours in the day, wasn't that the old cliché? Connor let out an empty laugh. For him, there were too many hours, too many hours where he went over and over his mistake, his past, and wished to God he could take everything back. He wished his wife was the soulful, interesting character she once was. He wished Caroline looked at him with passion burning in her eyes and she beckoned him to bed, or love shining in her tearful eyes when they had first realised she was pregnant. But no. She looked at him as if he was a distant creature, someone she looked at because it was her duty, not because she took pleasure from it. He wished…he wished…he wished... No! He threw his brandy glass at the wall, shards of glass splintering everywhere, the liquid trickling down the strong oak door. He breathed heavily…he could not keep wishing! Look where that got him last time? Living a life with woman who showed no emotion, who lived day by day with her façade of the caring wife. He knew if they could they would separate, and she would find some source of happiness. Just as he knew he'd be happier with a woman who made her enjoyment evident at being in his company. *You sound like a fool Connor, believing some woman would be with you after they found out about your past. The only woman you get is one who uses your status for her own personal gain.* He remembered his brother's words, after his first confession that he wanted a better life. His brother, John, had laughed, although not unkindly but as if he had been expecting it. How had he though? Connor was so sure of his disguise, so sure it covered all his true thoughts and characteristics that he was shocked when John had seen straight through the smoke screen. "You're not a sly as you think Con, sure to those posh totties out there who follow your every word you got them seeing what you want them to, but you forget, I'm your brother" Even now he could remember the cocksure grin John had worn afterwards, and how he had saluted him with his glass. Brothers….it didn't really mean much to Connor. Yes, the blood connection would always bind them, and if John needed him, he'd be there, but it would be out of duty, not out of brotherly love. Was that sad? He wondered, not many brothers had a relationship based on love or affection. But then, he mused, men would rarely show that love and affection they may feel. That would be seen as weak and God forbid a man being weak. How refreshing it would be to see emotion, even if it were weakness, no body could understand what he'd give to see his wife cry. How sad! He *wanted* his wife to cry, he wanted to witness her give into the sadness and pain she had bottled up since that fateful night. He wanted to see if she felt any remorse or grief. Hell, even after that night she hadn't seemed to have grieved properly. Would he feel the familiar guilt he always did when that night was mentioned? Or would he cry and break down with Caroline, finally allowing them to bond over a mutual sadness? "Oh stop with the questions fool!" He mumbled. Enough of the wishing and wondering and hoping, he'd had enough of the self inflicted torture. Caroline didn't make him feel the shame or guilt, she made him feel nothing. He laughed, a little hysterically, what a hollow and bleak existence his life was turning out to be!

Caroline Belle applied her red lipstick with a practiced hand. One swoop to the left, return to the centre, one swoop to the right and gently, ever so gently, bring the top and bottom lip together. Yes, she looked at herself with a smile that was better. She looked much more like herself now. She had no idea what had come over her! Rubbing at her head, smudging her perfectly applied face so that she had looked like a common tramp! Heaven forbid! She wore her blue jacket, the one which stopped just above her hip, and her fitted navy blue skirt, which showed enough leg to pry the men's eyes and to receive jealous looks from the women who walked past her. Yes, she did so love to show off her figure, she had always been told by her mother to "Use what ya got and flaunt it" She did heed the advice from her dearest mom, but did it in a classier way, rather than spreading her legs, flashing her assets at every man who entered the pub. Poor mom, she'd had so many men that night she didn't know which one could have been Caroline's father. She'd shown no remorse though, just stated it, as if it was the way of the world, and Caroline would have to "like it or lump it" as her mother used to say. Caroline had certainly "lumped" everything her mother threw at her over the years, if it wasn't for her mother… Dearest Mummy, she suddenly thought, all that cock she'd endured had finally hit a vital organ a few months ago. Oh not literally! Caroline laughed how funny *that* would've been! No dearest mummy had had a heart attack, sad for sure, but as she always used to say she'd have to "like it or lump it" Caroline smiled as her laughter died down, yes she'd certainly lumped it. Unlike Connor, Caroline had never wanted to feel affection for her mother, and never had. She'd been taught from the start how to hide her emotions, how to never, never let anyone know what she was thinking or what she wanted. Her mother had often commented it was best to give a fake name and a fake address. "They'll take advantage; they'll lift your skirts and start pumping away at ya like they're searching for something. All ya gotta do, love, is smile, sometimes give em the ol' "yes yes, give it to me hard, you big big stallion" routine, men love that girl" Another vital and important piece of advice her dearest mother had given her, and again, like before she'd done as she'd been told. She was fourteen when she'd first tried it; he'd paid her mum for the afternoon with her. Although she'd been young, she knew what to expect after growing up in the next room to her mother, hearing the same words she was told to repeat. The man who had taken her virginity had been so excited to have discovered he was her first, it had excited him so much he had came within the minute, and she hadn't even started her stallion routine yet. To say Caroline had been disappointed was an understatement, she'd been looking forward to it, to seeing his reactions to her words but no, he'd been too quick. There had been a few more in between, some cruel men her mother had sold her to, but they never lasted long enough for her to get into the "role" Until Connor. Caroline's small smile disappeared as she thought of her estranged husband. He'd been the first one she'd tried her routine out on, and he'd loved it, the pleasure at her words had been apparent on his face and Caroline was slightly miffed when he hadn't finished straight afterward. No, if she recalled correctly, he had just kept going, thumbing her clit until she had experienced her first orgasm. The moment had been an eye opener for her, she'd let herself go, had screamed and clawed with delight, she'd thrashed under him as his cock still pumped in and out of her wetness, he'd smiled, then grunted, and did one last thrust before he'd spilled his seed into her. Thinking back now, Caroline had genuinely enjoyed their first encounter and had been eager to do it again. For once she'd felt sexual pleasure, instead of just laying there while men used her, like so many had. She remembered herself being a passionate, wanton creature, using Connor as her testing dummy as she found out how far she could be taken. Caroline narrowed her eyes as she looked into the perfect face staring back at her in the mirror, Connor had held her back. She was capable of so many more things than her husband could imagine, and she would've experimented and discovered her limits, if she hadn't gotten pregnant. Her eyes widened in the mirror, she'd been so sad that day they'd realised she was with child that she had cried. Her life had ended. "Ya don't wanna get up the duff little girl, cos' if ya do, kiss goodbye to yer freedom and sexuality, nothing like pushing a baby through yer pussy to put you off having a cock in there" Caroline flinched as her mothers harsh words rumbled through her mind, as if spoken aloud. Her mother's crassness had never, thankfully, influenced Caroline to speak like that. She wouldn't have the life she did now if she spoke those words in public. No, she reserved language like that for special times only, depending on who her partner was and what he desired. Today her client preferred the colour blue, so she wore blue, he preferred high heels, so she wore high heels, he liked her hair up and so she wore it up. Anything he desired, she did for him.

A sudden smash startled her. She spun around on her chair to see if Connor had entered the room, but no of course he couldn't have. She sighed with relief and turned back to the mirror. She didn't necessarily like keeping her husband distant, but it was a necessity. Both of their past's were intertwined to such a degree that neither of them could escape without causing a commotion for him and his career or herself. On some level Caroline felt safe being trapped in a marriage, she had the power. She held the key to ruin Connor's career and damn him to a life of true loneliness. Yes, if the world discovered what happened that night, it would be over for both of them. They were bound together by a secret, one that had to remain within their marriage. She liked to keep him on his toes by threatening to let the world know their past. It was funny, she thought as she stood and straightened her jacket, they didn't connect or share anything in common anymore, but the one thing they could agree on, was the importance of appearances.

"Come now, let's compare our pain." Charles smirked, tapping his chin, "It's obvious you want everyone to view you with a sympathetic eye." He continued, regarding the woman sitting across from him "'Cos let's face it, that defiantly going to get you the award" He turned away to look out the window and sighed. What would he give to see a beautiful calming view instead of the polluted, grey dismal scene London appeared to be these days.
"I don't want people to know about my past" Scarlet Windsor said from where she sat. Charles turned to look at her, almost missing what she said as she spoke in a very unassuming way. She was sometimes too quiet for her own good, people would take advantage of her if she didn't speak up and show the confidence she had somewhere in her. *Who are you kidding? You're using her like every other agent in the world.* Yes, maybe he was, but Charles shouldn't feel guilty, it was the way of the world. People took advantage and used what they could to further themselves. It was just the way it was. Although looking at Scarlet and her kind, loving face, her red hair pinned up showing her slightly angular facial structure, he couldn't help but feel a twinge of something. Remorse? Guilt? He didn't know. He felt desire for sure, Scarlet was without a doubt, a breathtaking woman. She was one of those rare breeds who was beautiful, and who knew it, but didn't use it. It had been a long time since Charles had encountered a woman such as Scarlet, her rich red hair and name gave

the impression of a fiery character, but she was as gentle as anything. *That's her downfall,* he reminded himself. He shook himself, knowing what he had to do and wishing he could get to the point.

"Scarlet" he sighed her name and he returned to his chair and sat opposite her. "You must've known that your past was going to get out. You're a freaking celebrity! You should have told me so I could have prepared a defence. Instead I learn about your abandonment through a tabloid dickhead, while he was shoving a microphone in my face." He cracked his knuckles while regarding her, "and all you do is refuse to talk. Now either this is a publicity stunt, I know you didn't get the part in that movie, but you needn't worry I would've sorted you out, or this is genuine, which as much as it pains me, still creates a problem"

"Why would it cause a problem if it was a genuine mistake? I mean surely it's better if it were an accident"

Scarlet looked at Charlie across the table, she knew what was coming, so why didn't the weasel just come out and say it? She didn't understand why no one would cut her some slack; she was just as surprised to see those pictures and headlines as anybody else was.

"Because, darling," Scarlet held in a wince, she hated it when he called her that "it was a part of your contract for me to know everything, and I mean everything about your past" he breathed heavily as if the whole world was on his shoulders "I don't know what to tell you, you blatantly ignored a stipulation of a contract, and if this occurs, which it has, I have every right to…remove you from our list"

Inwardly Scarlet laughed, ah yes, so he did know what to tell her, but he was giving her the I'm-at-a-loss-at-what-to-do look. Why was she so surprised? It's "the way of the world". So, here she was again, trying to keep her past a secret to help her, but it always kept creeping up behind her, ruining everything the moment her life was good. She was aware that Charlie had taken his usual stance by the window, it must make him feel important, she thought as she smoothed her skirt down to below her knee. She didn't like the way he looked at her, as if he'd like to devour her bit by bit, it reminded her of the way her mother's boyfriends had always looked at her. To say the least, it gave her the creeps, she smiled, yes the creeps, so simple to explain but the feelings it provoked were much more serious. Whenever a man looked at her that way, old feelings of disgust and hatred bubbled up inside her, making her shake with the violence of it. She felt sick in her own skin, making her want to claw at herself, wanting to escape this body she had. Sure, some would say she was lucky for a small, slim, toned body, and yes she was grateful for it as it had helped her with her career, as no one would want a fat actress, but to Scarlet, it was such a burden, sometimes she felt like wanting to run away and hide.

"The abandonment" as Charlie so nicely put it, was much more complicated and heart breaking than the tabloids could ever convey. They always only came up with half the story, and surprise surprise, it was the half that either gave her sympathy or made her out to be the bad guy. The truth of her past was rather simple, but aftermath was what made it complicated. Her mum was never as attentive or loving as she should have been. Scarlet remembered her as a stick figure with a bottle of Gin in one hand and a fag in the other. Her mother, Lily, was a gorgeous woman in her younger years and would have still been sparkling in her elder years if she hadn't abused her body with alcohol. Scarlet realised now that her mother's need for booze was the result of her loneliness which was surprising considering the many boyfriends she'd had. Scarlet's childhood was lived in a blur of parties, many different men coming and going, arguments, the sounds of glass smashing and her mum coming into her bedroom and collapsing in the bed they shared. Their house, or more accurately, their caravan, was amidst many other families going through the same motions. It wasn't all bad, Scarlet realised now, as her and her mum were always on the move with the other caravan families, so she met many different people and went to many different schools, seeing a lot for her young age. As a child Scarlet had thought it all a big exciting adventure, changing homes as often as her mum changed boyfriends, but it wasn't until one day at her new school, a young boy at pointed at her and said "Gypsy". She remembered now that the room had gone silent, all eyes on her, and that was the very first time she had wanted to claw out of her own skin. As it turned out, that boy had only been the beginning of the horrible future that had been laid ahead for her.

Snapping herself out of her memories, she forced herself to concentrate on Charlie, and accepted that she wasn't going to be represented by this company anymore.

"It's fine" clearing her throat she stood up and looked at Charlie "I understand I failed to honour the terms of our agreement, and I'm sorry if I have caused you or the company any problems. If you'll excuse me now" she started away towards the door, but Charlie stood in front of her. He was a few feet away but Scarlet would

have preferred him back over at his window, where he looked down on everyone out of it.
"Is that it? I mean come on Darling; would it kill ya to show some emotion? To shout, scream, even perhaps" he stepped closer "beg me to keep you on"
She calmly took a breathed as the stench of garlic mushrooms wafted into her face, great she thought; at least I know what he had for lunch.
"Look, Charlie-"
"Yes I love it when you call me that"
"- I do appreciate everything you've done, but as you say I must be let go-" Charlie put his hand on her arm, urging her to take a step towards him "So I suggest you let me go" she added.
"I know I have to let you go, in the business sense, but not in the personal sense" He leaned forward, his hand idly rubbing her wrist and his eyes danced over her face "Come on Scar, you know you wanna…extend our contract?"
For Scarlet, she'd have liked to say it was the cheesy comment he said, but it was the wiggle of his bushy eyebrows that really made her feel angry.
"Look," she snapped, pulling her wrist away from his grasp "I don't want to be with you in that sense; I have never, ever, given you that impression"
Charlie looked a bit bemused by her outburst, Scarlet wasn't sure if it was her show of anger, which she rarely let anyone see, or her comment that she didn't want him.
"But, all the chicks dig me" he protested, dropping his arms and looking at her with a hurt expression.
Normally Scarlet would've felt bad at causing someone sadness, as she knew what that felt like, but all that the

hurt expression on his face did, was rise her ire even more.
"Oh for God's sake! First of all, we're not "chicks" we hate it when you call us that. Second of all, "Dig?" please you're not nineteen. And third of all, No we don't all like you that way, jeeze, can't a girl just be nice to a man without him expecting sex in return?"
The silence that greeted her in return was enough to let her know he was shocked, and to be honest, so was she. Scarlet never lost control of her emotions like that she was pretty good at hiding her feelings, hell, she had to considering what business she was in. As she pondered what had come over her, Charles walked back over to the window, keeping his eyes firmly on the people below. Why had he propositioned her? He knew she wouldn't take him up on it so why had he embarrassed himself? Damn her! She did this! Her and that body of hers put him under a spell; making him act like an idiot, well screw her! What does she expect going around wearing tarty skirts and flimsy blouses?
"I think you need to re-think your wardrobe if you don't want men's attentions" he said quietly, turning around to her, "If you think wearing that" he gestured to her clothes "outfit isn't going to get a man testosterone going up, then you can take your naive little mind and get the hell out of my office!" They stared at each other, and then slowly Scarlet walked to the door and went through it. Ha he had gotten what he wanted! She was gone and he'd made his point...he was on….he stopped looking out the window when he heard laughing voices outside his office, he stomped over, wondering what was going on and opened the door to face some of his work colleagues smiling and laughing.
"What? What is so funny?" he demanded. When they

sniggered some more, one of them crooned "Oooo I love it when you call me Charlie", Charles' face turned red as he heard "Want some garlic mushrooms boss?" He looked around for Scarlet, intending to give her a piece of his mind, when he saw her looking at him from the open elevator. If Charles wasn't as angry, he would've admitted it was pretty smooth when she gave him a finger wave as the elevator doors shut.

Chapter Two

Caroline dressed appropriately for her client, taking into consideration his likes and dislikes. He was very particular about the details surrounding their encounters. Firstly, that she referred to him as Mr. Black. This stipulation had confused Caroline, as in her experience most men had preferred her to croon their names with desire. But as Mr. Black had proven time and time again, he was not like most men. Their sexual experiences ranged from the fierce and powerful to the dominant and submissive. Oh, how Mr. Black loved it when she surrendered to his demands, doing as he wished with a smile on her face.

As she walked down the corridor to the hotel room, she knew what would be waiting for her, she had dressed coyly for the occasion, knowing how he would react to the shy, innocent act he loved so much. She knocked, waited, then the door opened with a fierce gush hitting her in the face.

"Yes?" he demanded, eyebrows drawn together.

Caroline raised an eyebrow and slowly trailed her eyes over his body. Starting with his rugged, handsome face, which bore the tails of his harsh life experiences, then to his broad shoulders which lead to his magnificently muscled arms, oh how they supported her weight when he held her against the wall while taking her roughly! Her appraisal continued down onto his flat stomach, concealed by a white crisp shirt, then to the outline of his obviously aroused cock, down to his strong thighs, leading further down to his muscled legs. Of course, she knew each curve and hollow of his body, she'd seen and used it enough times to, but even with clothes on, any normal woman would notice his body. She

stepped around him, not uttering a word, she knew how he reacted to the prolonged silences between them, and she knew how the sexual tensions heighten because of it. She glanced around the room, noting the different objects but only really looking for the bed. When she'd spotted it she turned back to Mr. Black and stood unassumingly, waiting for his next comment. She wore her buttoned up coat, one that concealed nothing from below her knee to the top of her neck. It was his turn to look her up and down, eyes narrowed he stalked purposely towards her, until they were a breath apart. "Undress for me." He demanded. A tingle of excitement tickled its down Caroline's spine, she did so love it when he took charge. She threw her bag on the floor next to her, and raising her gaze to his, slowly began undoing each button, one at a time, deliberately making him wait.
"Quicker" he said, now staring at her fingers, watching their movements closely. She bit her lip, as he took over undressing her.
"But…Mr. Black, I was doing as you asked…" her words trailed off as she watched him finish his task and return to looking at her face.
"You didn't do it fast enough. When I say for you to do something, I mean for you to do it" She could see the retrained sexual desire in his eyes, building and building, and she couldn't help but want it to explode.
"I'm sorry Mr. Black" she hung her head in shame "Maybe I can do something to…make it up to you"
"Yes, yes you can. You can suck my dick"
Her head snapped up, a false look of shock on her face "But…I don't do such things, Mr Black, I am far too innocent to even conceive that…perverse act"

“I told you, when I tell you to do something I expect you to do it” he grabbed her hair and pulled her closer, “and I expect you to suck my cock, now on your knees in front of me”

She regarded him for a moment, feeling her body respond to his rough manner, she could feel the answering wetness between her thighs and secretly longed for him to thrust his magnificent cock inside her, until she came apart. But Mr. Black enjoyed these games, and he was after all, a pay client.

Without answering she bent down to her knees and unzipped his trousers. His fully aroused cock sprang free from its confides, jutting out proudly from the midst of brown hair which curled around it. She sighed with pleasure; oh she did love this part of him.

She wrapped her fingers around it one by one, applying pressure periodically, just the way he liked it.

“Enough. Put it in your mouth and suck it. Hard” he added, to confirm any queries she might have had. Like she needed telling what to do to please him! She knew what he liked better than he did. She obliged him, flicking her tongue out to taste him, before placing the head of his cock inside her mouth and sucking, while using her tongue to lick the slit at the top. He moaned and yanked her head harder, shoving his dick further down her throat. She didn’t mind, she loved having as much as she could of him.

“Touch yourself. Touch yourself while sucking my dick” He ordered, his nails digging into the back of head. Caroline hiked her skirt with her free hand, thankful for not wearing any underwear. Her fingers sought her wet, slick entrance and a jolt went through her when she found her clit. She rubbed it in a circular motion, moaning around his cock, the sound vibrating, causing Mr. Black to moan once again.

"Are your fingers in you pussy?" he asked. All Caroline could do was moan in response as she dipped her index finger into her tight, wet, tunnel.

"Yeah, you're touching yourself, thinking of me shoving my dick inside your pussy" he moaned as she increased the pressure of her fingers "Yeah, just like that, squeeze me hard, squeeze me like your wet pussy will"

Caroline increased her pace, feeling incredibly aroused, just needing to reach some release. Mr. Black always had this effect on her, allowing herself to express her passionate nature that Connor thought long dead in her. Suddenly, Mr. Black lifted her by her arms and threw her onto the bed; He strode towards her and ripped her skirt from her body, leaving her bare. She noticed his eyes flamed even more when he realised she hadn't worn any underwear. His face was contorted with desire, flames burning in the depths of his eyes. He brought her to a sitting position and kneeling next to her, he pulled her head down to continue her ministrations from earlier.

A gasp escaped him at the renewed contact, but this time he didn't let it continue as long as before, he pushed her down, grabbed her breast, flicking the nipple with his finger, then leant forward to suck on it. At the same time he pushed himself into her wet pussy, making them both gasp at the sensation.

"Oh god…you feel so…wet and tight." He took a breath "God, you're so wet for me aren't you?"

"Oh yes, yes you turn me on so much"

He started to thrust in and out of her, and continued this steady rhythm until Caroline couldn't bear it anymore.
"Please just…please"
"What? What do you want me to do to you?"
"Just…oh God…pound me hard, just fuck me!"
Mr. Black gave an unsteady laugh. "If you insist" He then braced his hands on her hips, and raised himself high above her and drove deep into her core, shuddering at the sensation. He continued this frenzied pace, driving hard and deep, the tightness of her pussy gripping his cock, until she could feel herself coming apart, she could feel the tension building and building. Then suddenly she exploded with a strangled cry, the sensations overwhelming her, the waves of ecstasy rippling over her body. A moment later, Mr. Black shouted as he came, joining her in the sensations that consumed them both. He laid a top of her, catching his breath, while she smoothed his hair out of his face. Mr. Black didn't look at her as he got up and went to the bathroom to clean, he left Caroline lying there, naked and spent. She rose on an elbow, looking at the door he'd gone through and sighed. Her smile was one of self mockery as she thought about her situation. Connor thought her unfeeling and cold and she was when they were together, she had realised this is because she felt trapped. Yet, when she was with Mr. Black she felt free to explore her passionate nature. How could she feel so trapped with one brother, but feel so free with the other?

"Knock knock! Anyone there?" Busty Blackburn's voice yelled through the door. Scarlet inwardly sigh, she did not have the energy to deal with Busty tonight.

"Ooo come on girl, let me in, I have no balls because they've frozen off!" Her distinguished laughter boomed along the empty hallway. Busty was known for her energetic, likeable although sometimes slightly crude jokes, and her ability to put a positive spin on any problem. However, Scarlet was in no mood to be given a motivational speech by Busty, sometimes she just wanted to wallow in misery for a while. Why was it so hard to do that?

Nevertheless she answered the door and plastered a smile on her face, which was the one she usually reserved for photographs. With one look at Scarlet, Busty shook her head her lips pursing with disapproval. "Listen, what did we agree on? There's to be no bullshit between us!" Despite her mood, Scarlet did genuinely smile. It was true, five years ago Scarlet and Busty had both been introduced at a PR gathering and had quickly bonded over a mutual dislike of meaningless small talk. Scarlet supposed that's why they had quickly become friends after that, both agreeing to speak their minds, and to tell the truth if something or someone was bothering them, even if it was each other.

"I know" Scarlet smiled and stepped aside. Busty needing no further invitation, swept past her, knowing her way around Scarlet's modest flat. Even though most people would think it crazy for her to live in a small flat, considering the money she had at her disposal, but she had always preferred smaller places, she felt more cosy and safe than if she lived on her own in a mansion. Busty, who also lived on her own, had a completely different opinion. She thought it best to spend what she had while she had it. "I take life by the balls...or wait is it supposed to be horns?" she'd once said, causing them both to burst into laughter. Scarlet did admire her attitude, for she had always wished she could take more risks and just live life each day at a time. But, it just wasn't in her character to do so, instead she had her pension plan all sorted out and her will was regularly updated when she came into any more money or property. She watched Busty as she uncorked the wine she'd brought with her and doubted Busty even knew what a pension plan was.

"Right, so you need to tell me all about how your past got out, 'cos I swear girl, I didn't tell a single soul. I know you get all freaky when that is mentioned. So it depends on who else you told" she paused as she contemplated the bottle "And if you want, I'll rough 'em up for ya"

Scarlet wrapped her arms around herself "I don't know, I haven't told anyone else, but to be honest, Bust, that's not even my main concern"

"Really?" Busty handed her a glass of wine, moving to the sofa, where they both sat, "What's worse than having pictures of your mama and gypsy mates on the front page?"

"Well, when you put it like that…"

Busty winced "I'm sorry, you know I can't do the soft and gentle crap, but ok, let me try again." She took a breath and elegantly crossed her legs, her hands joined on her knees "Please tell me what's going on, Darling?"

There was a moment's silence, where they started at each other, then cracked up in laughter. "Oh…God…" Scarlet gasped between breaths "Please go back….go back to…being yourself"

Busty laughed heartily while wiping her eyes, "Oh yes please, I felt uncomfortable saying that"

"Oh I don't know Bust," Scarlet said on a sigh "Charlie dumped me two days ago"
Busty looked at her with sharp eyes "Wait, you mean you were doing each other? What did I tell you! God never EVER get involved-"
"I'm not having sex with him!"
She stopped in mid-sentence and looked at Scarlet, relief crossing her face. "Well good, you know how I feel about those types of relationships" Yes, she knew all about Busty's bad relationship with her manager a few years ago. It was the first and only time that Scarlet knew of where Busty had been in love, madly and passionately in love, which ended horribly and very publicly when his affair with a fellow actress was splashed all over the front page of the news. It was the first time Scarlet had seen her cry, and she was sure it would be the last time if Busty could help it. She felt uncomfortable when people saw her vulnerability, which is why, Scarlet suspected, she tried hard to always show her happy, positive side. It was safer that way.
"No, don't worry, it was nothing like that. I meant he "dumped" me as in pushed me off the agents books."
"They can't do that!"
"Yeah, they can because apparently I didn't fulfil my agreement in letting them know my full past history"
Busty physically balked at her comment. Outraged, she poured herself another glass of wine, noted that Scarlet hadn't touched hers, she never did though, and lifted the rim to her lips. "Well I can tell you that they are so full of bullshit, I hate agents!"
"Yeah so do I" Scarlet muttered
"Hmm, you know what you should do, publicly call them on it"

"No…because then it will just put more focus on why I'm doing it, therefore more God damned questions about my past."

"Yeah, I guess you're right, but jeeze, they do annoy me"

They fell into a companionable silence, both left to their own thoughts. Scarlet thought about her friend sitting next to her. She wondered how deeply those scares ran beneath her hard exterior, and felt sudden rage against the man who had done it all. But, unlike Busty, she knew there was no point in offering to "rough 'em up" for her. She couldn't do it even if she was asked to, God sometimes she hated herself for feeling so weak! That familiar sickening feeling began to build up inside her; she began to recognise the sensations even before they took root. *Oh please no, not now,* she silently begged to herself. She didn't want to feel this way, she didn't want to feel as if she had to escape her own body. Her skin began to feel heavy and clammy, ugh! No she hated the feel of her skin. *No, don't let it win, calm down, deep breath.*

In an effort to quench this sickening feeling, Scarlet rose and walked to the kitchen, on the pretence of getting a glass of water.

"You know, I got a number for you" Busty yelled from the sofa. Scarlet took a breath and wiped a wet wash cloth over her forehead.

"Oh yeah?" was all she could manage to reply without her voice breaking.

"Yeah, ever heard of Connor Belle?"

Slowly, the feeling began to subside, allowing Scarlet to dimly note what Busty was saying. She had heard of the name before, but couldn't place him in her current state.

"Um, I think so, who is he again?"
"Well," she could hear Busty place her wine glass down on the table "he is also in the same business as Charles, but of course better than he is. He doesn't come cheap; in fact some people say his prices are way too high"
"Is he really that good then to have high prices?"
"Well, yes" Busty stopped talking and Scarlet could hear her rustling through her bag "well, I suppose, there have been rumours that the reason why he prices himself so high is because he doesn't actually want clients."
This gave Scarlet pause. What PR agent didn't want clients? "Why?" She had the impression of Busty shrugging when she said "Who knows? It seems he never makes an effort to gain new clients, and I've been told he doesn't appear overly bothered if he doesn't get the client."
Scarlet returned to the lounge, finally losing the rest of those dreadful feelings. She looked at Busty who smiled at her as she helped herself to another generous glass of wine.
"Hmm, that is a bit odd for someone not to want clients, especially when his choice of business is so competitive."
"Well, like I say, he doesn't seem to care really. He'll do the work if he gets the client of course, but even then he always gives them a good amount of leeway." Busty suddenly smiled "that's probably why he's so popular, no actress or singer wants a PR agent breathing down their necks"
Scarlet had to smile at that as well, as it was the reason she'd be employing Connor Belle as well.

"Why do I recognise his name?" she asked Busty who was busy studying her nails.
She looked up, "Well you must've heard of the tragedy he and his wife suffered a years back?" when Scarlet looked clueless Busty continued "His wife is Caroline Belle, a nutcase if you ask me, but anyone would feel sympathy for her when they lost their child. Apparently a burglar had broken into the house and attacked Caroline, you see she was eight months pregnant at the time, he apparently threw her down the stairs, savagely I'm told, leaving her for dead. Meanwhile, Connor is unaware of what's happening while he's still at work. He gets home to find Caroline nearly dead and blood pouring out of her…well you know. So, they go to the hospital, where they're told their child is dead, and that somehow she had damaged her…well I'm not sure what she damaged, but it stopped her from ever having children again. They were devastated as they only got married 'cos she was pregnant in the first place. To be perfectly frank, I'm surprised they've even last this long! A lot of people thought they'd split after, but they seem to have hung on." Busty finished her glass of wine and put it on the table "Mind you, I've gotta say they don't look like the perfect couple-oh on the outside they do, but I've seen them at a few parties where they thought no one was watching them. Connor had looked pretty angry, while Caroline remained cool and calm, I'm telling you, she needs to pull that stick out of her arse."
Scarlet smile, although it didn't reach her eyes "Maybe Caroline just doesn't like public events so she uses an act, like we do"

Busty looked at her friend and smiled sadly. "You've always gotta make it that no one's in the wrong. You're kind girl, but annoying"

"All I'm saying is that we have no idea how losing her baby and being told she can't have anymore would have affected her."

"No I know that, but, when I look at her, I get the chills, it's as if she never really cared, there's just some cold emotion in her eyes that makes me doubt she feels anything"

Scarlet's eyebrows snapped together "Oh come on, you can't seriously believe she feels nothing! I mean of course she feels something; otherwise she'd be pure evil. She just expresses her emotions differently; it doesn't mean she has none"

Busty remained quiet after her outburst, then finally said in a quiet voice, "Scar, who are you trying to convince?"

Scarlet's eyes snapped to her friend "No one, I just mean that if she is incapable of feeling then she is more dangerous. She is human after all"

Again Busty remained silent, looking at Scarlet, silently conveying the comment she was about to say. Scarlet knew it was coming, how many times had it cropped up before?

"Your mother had feelings Scarlet, she did love you, but I think in her mind she was doing you a favour by leaving you on that camp site"

"Don't…"

"Look, I know I'm wrong to say Caroline has no feelings, but when you see her for the first time, look into her eyes. They're flat and cold, there's no warmth there. But no, I guess you are right, she does have emotions, she just expresses them differently" Busty

stood, gathering her bag "Look I gotta go, I got a hot date tonight, so I'm going to my wax and stylist"
Scarlet rose to "At this hour?"
Busty laughed "Yeah sure, a girl's gotta be prepared!" they both walked to the door when Busty turned back to grab Scarlet in a hug. "You know I'm here for you, you were loved by your mother and you're loved by me"
Scarlet returned the hug, needing the support, liking the way Busty could read her and know she was thinking of her mother and her heartless abandonment. She shut the door behind Busty and leant on it. How could a mother just leave her child? While she was at school, how could a mother just clear her things and leave the camp site they had lived on? It was something she couldn't understand, but she knew for sure that if she ever had a child, she would be incapable of leaving it behind, alone and defenceless, as her mother had done to her.

Connor was meeting one of his many existing clients. She was pretty, slim and possessed eyes of a seductress. But she was also lacking anything between her ears. To be honest, he thought as he gazed down at her file his assistant had handed to him, he couldn't even remember her name. Why, when he put his prices to maximum limit, fobbed actresses and actors off with excuses, did they continue to come and pester him? A long while ago, when he had finally decided he had to get away from Caroline and the hold she had over him, he had accepted he would have to end his career. But, he wanted to do it slowly, quietly, so he didn't arouse suspicions from the media or his ice queen of a wife. So he had started this plan, to put his prices up, to become suddenly "unavailable", but all this plan had achieved was making his clients follow and try to persuade him more frequently. Did they not think he had a life? He would have laughed if it wasn't so sad when it occurred to him that actually, he in fact did *not* have a life. He couldn't help the bitterness and pain that built up inside him when he thought of the reasons as to why that was true. The innocent part he had played that night, only came back to haunt him, and he without a doubt, blamed his wife for his loneliness and sadness. But then, he couldn't think like that could he? No he couldn't because when he thought about it, he was never going to be rid of Caroline, so it was in his best interest to continue letting everyone, including her, that he was content.

No matter how far that was from the truth.

He shook himself, thinking if he was to keep up his charade, then he ought to start listening to this…uh…actress in front of him.

He leant back, casually allowing his arms to rest in his lap. "Well, I got that magazine interview for you, miss…uh miss"

She graced him with a grateful, sunny smile. "Oh my God, like, thank you and all that. You have no idea what this, like, means to me. This mag was one of my fav's as a young girl"

He looked at her through narrowed eyes "Young girl? Honey, you are young"

She laughed, and Connor resisted the urge to flinch at the insincerity that rang to it. "Yes, I am twenty, but I am getting on in the years"

Hmm, having a twenty year old say that to him, a man of forty-three, did nothing to reassure him he still had time left for happiness. No, he brought himself up sharply, he would not think of his real life when he was acting a part of a world where reality and sincerity did not exist. He wondered why and how he had tolerated this business for so long, when he truly despised it, but once again he had Caroline to thank for this particular entrapment.

"Well, anyway, nice seeing you again, miss. Give me a call and let me know how you got on"

She, whoever she was, pouted unhappily. "You won't be there Connor? PR agents are supposed to be there surely?"

Damn. "Yes, usually they are, I'll try to, but I think I'm away for a few nights next week, either way, just be yourself" not too much though, he thought "and you'll do perfectly"

She smiled at him. "Yes, I will be fine won't I?"

He nodded and opened the door, resisting the urge to all but push her out of it. He returned to his seat to contemplate the agony of doing something he hated. It was why Caroline probably threatened him with revealing their secret, to keep him in a job he hated. But no, he shook his head, his act of being the happy PR agent was too convincible for her to see through....wasn't it?

"Mr Belle will see you now" Scarlet looked up from the book she was reading to the pretty receptionist standing before her. She smiled politely and followed her to the office, where presumably the famous Mr. Belle sat, no doubt behind his big oak desk with one of those fake, charming smiles on his face. Yes, some would say she was cynical when it came to the media, or representatives of it, but who could seriously read the headlines these days and believe any of it? She did wish she could embrace the media and make the tabloids dance to her tune, as Busty did, but she just couldn't tolerate the slyness and the dishonesty that existed within the industry.

Oh, no time to dwell on it now, the bottom line was, she was an actress who attracted the media, so she'd have to find someone who would deal with it better than she could.

And who better than Mr. Belle?

Scarlet stepped around the receptionist, murmured her thanks, and found herself staring at a man standing in the same place as Charlie had. Looking out the window, his arms joined at his back, his face arrested with a thoughtful expression. She barely suppressed a snort, thoughtful? Where people like him capable of being thoughtful?

Nevertheless, Scarlet chose her most dazzling smile and approach Mr. Belle.

"Mr. Belle?" she extended her hand as he turned to her "it's a pleasure to meet you. I can not explain how much I've been looking forward to this meeting"

Mr. Belle looked slightly surprised to see her, and regarded her hand with a confused look, before seeming to gather himself together and shake her hand. He met her eyes, and she found herself looking into the most piercing pairs of blue eyes she'd ever encountered. They were stunningly clear, and held a hints of wisdom and sadness, but she must have imagined it, as the emotions where gone as quick as they came.

"It's good to meet you…uh…miss" he said and released her hand and sat down, gesturing her to do the same opposite him.

"Please, let's not be so formal, call me Scarlet"

He looked surprised by her request, but quickly recovered and smiled at her. "Yes, you're right. Then you must call me Connor"
She returned his smile "Great"
They sat in silence for a few beats before she noticed Connor looked at her blankly, as if he were trying to remember what they were here to discuss. Maybe he had forgotten, after all, most PR agents wouldn't survive without their receptionist's or "right hand man" Typical, her cynical opinion was once more proven correct.
"I see you have forgotten why I am here" she said on a sigh.
"Uh...no I haven't, I am sorry, my mind was elsewhere"
"Elsewhere? That's encouraging for the line of profession you're in" she replied coolly, letting him know she was not impressed. But when she expected him to scowl at her or deny her claim, once again his face showed surprise, and then, although she wasn't for certain, she thought she saw a little humour in his eyes before it disappeared.
"Hmm, I can see I'll have my hands full with you, um...uh, Scarlet, but as you have pointed out, I haven't got the best mind for this type of profession, anymore of course"
She started blankly at him, unsure if she knew what he was trying to say.
"So, you're probably better off choosing someone who can do your talent justice, and give you the proper publicity you deserve" For the second time in their short meeting, Scarlet found herself sitting in silent, staring at the man across from her. He didn't want her business? *No* PR agent didn't want business, so she

wondered if he had heard about her past, perhaps that's why he didn't wish to take her on.
"I do realise my…past has put somewhat of a strain on my career at the moment, but I was assured by a friend that your skills in publicity would help me get back into the public eye with dignity and subtly"
Connor chuckled a little at her comment, a small chuckle which insinuated he thought her words naive.
"Scarlet…there is no such thing as entering the public eye with dignity or subtly, please do yourself a favour and stop kidding yourself"
His arrogance irritated her to no end. "I believe it can be done with the right agent. And I believe you are the right agent for me and my needs"
Connor sat forward, his hands in front of him and laced his fingers. "I think it's safer to say that you're "needs" would be better off in the hands of someone else"
She shook her head "No, I have been told that you have dealt with problems such as…unsavoury past lives before"
"And who, may I ask, told you this?"
"My close friend, Busty Blackburn" she announced the name proudly, sure it would have some effect on this arrogant PR agent.
He looked at her blankly, his expression appearing rather bored. "Well, anyway, I'm flattered your friend Busty would hold me in such high regards, but I truly can not put more emphasis on the fact that you would be better off with someone else"
Scarlet looked at him. But this time she really looked at Connor Belle, deciding she needed to figure this guy out. Yes, he spoke with arrogance, she wouldn't have expected anything less with a PR agent, but it was his continuous effort to return to his first comment that she

should find someone else. Why? Yes her past was an annoyance, but it wasn't awful like drugs or prostitution that other actresses have been known to confess to. So why was she so different? Jeeze, anyone would think he didn't want her business!
She was insulted, but at the same time, strangely disappointed. She thought Mr. Belle-Connor-was truly her way out of this mess. She studied him; taking note of the shabby and crinkled suit he wore, looking nearly as old as he, which now she thought about it, he looked about forty. His unshaven jaw held the beginnings of shadow, adding emphasis to his facial structure. Now that she thought about it, the unshaven jaw added to his features quite well, giving him a slightly dangerous and mysterious quality. Again she was drawn to his blue eyes, fringed with thick black lashes, an odd combination she thought absently. Then she took in his hair, slightly overgrown, hanging loosely down his face. Mind you, she thought her gaze returning to his eyes, his hair didn't look awful at all; in fact Connor Belle was rather handsome, in a roughened type of way.
His eyes locked with hers, and they gave nothing away. Interesting she thought, that he could mask all his emotions and reduce those beautiful eyes to a appearing flat and uninterested. No, she suddenly realised, there's much more to this man. She could sense the tension in his body and the many emotions he was probably suppressing.
"Now, that you are done inspecting me, Scarlet, perhaps we can get back to the matter at hand?"
She couldn't help herself, she blushed, something she hadn't done since she was a child.

"I wasn't "inspecting" you; I was merely looking at the man who is insulting me and my career, by declining my kind offer of representing me"

He looked as if he might smile "You're rather sure of yourself aren't you?"

Scarlet frowned "How so?"

"Well," Connor leant back and casually regarded her, although Scarlet could tell there was nothing casual about this man "You assume your offer is kind, which obviously means you think your career is one of great consequence." He raised an eyebrow at her "And you assume I would jump at the chance of representing you, slightly arrogant don't you think?" this time Connor Belle did smile. A small smug smile, which angered Scarlet. She suspected she was angry because what he said was right, but it didn't mean she had to accept that. Of all the nerve! Him calling her arrogant?

She forced a careless laugh, her eyes narrowing at him, and to think she thought him handsome a minute ago!

"Well, forgive me Mr. Belle-"

"Please, call me Connor"

"-but if you are so willing to turn people away, such as I, then I can't help but think you need all the business you can get. Surely you don't believe that by refusing my business it will help you?"

He shrugged "It would cause me less work and trouble"

Scarlet's laugh this time was bitter. "I forgot PR agents don't like hard work, only the rewards, but you forget Mr. Belle that you have a nice little receptionist out there"

He frowned, looking confused "What's that got to do with anything?"

"Well, of course you people usually just give them the work, and take all the credit," Scarlet sneered at him "I do hope you are paying her well for enduring your company each day"

This time, Connor couldn't help himself, he laughed. He laughed so loudly and heartily he clutched his sides to prevent it from hurting. She was a fierce little woman! How refreshing, he thought, to be talked to like that. He'd hoped to irritate her enough with his arrogant, uncaring attitude, so that she would walk out. But, God, she was persistent. His laughter died down; oh she was going to be a problem. One he seemed to be enjoying too much already.

He sat forward again and looked at her. She looked slightly uncomfortable at his burst of laughter, but he couldn't care. How good it felt to laugh again after so long!

"You're quite right" she looked at him suspiciously when he said that and he suppressed a smile. "I do put a certain amount of work on my receptionist, she is a great help to me, and don't worry yourself, Pam is well paid for her effort" He was glad when Scarlet had the grace to blush again, he found himself wanting to really give her something to blush about. Maybe a kiss, or a slight touch-*woah*! Where had these thoughts appeared from? Connor didn't do the flirting thing anymore, not since that night with Caroline. He shook his head at looked at Scarlet. She was a stunning woman, absolutely stunning. Shame she wouldn't look at him twice, and even if she did-he couldn't exactly do anything about it…could he?

"Well, I am glad to hear that" her voice shook him out of his thoughts and back to the matter at hand.

"Because you are so very adamant that I take you on, I will-for a trial period. When I do an awful job of fixing

your…career, you'll fire me anyway, but if it's a risk you want to take, then just say yes"
Scarlet paused before agreeing. Connor was so sure he'd fail; she had to wonder if he deliberately intended to fail, but then it occurred to her, just having his name associated with hers would do the world of good. For some reason his successful reputation was solid, no matter what he did now to affect that.
"Yes"
They looked at each other, not quite sure what either of them had agreed to.

John Belle strode through the restaurant, his eyes trained on his guest awaiting him. To the casual observer, it would seem he didn't notice anyone or anything outside of his line of vision. Of course, anyone who knew the real John Belle would know that he was aware of everything around him. It was rumoured he had eyes in the back of his head, that he knew people's moves before they knew themselves. He was a man who everyone tired to get on his good side for having him on your bad side would surely mean your life would be unpleasant. People often wondered what his appeal was to women, but it was a well known fact that he took women one each night, even two at a time. Even though his appearance was rugged, his face angular, marred by a deep scar beginning at his mouth, and ending at the tip of his right eyebrow, he was well sought by the female population, his talents infamous, as no woman left his bed unsatisfied. However, not everyone knew the full story concerning his choice of women, only those who were close to him, which unsurprisingly, were only a few. One of which was his brother, Connor Belle.

If only Connor knew what John did with Caroline, perhaps they wouldn't be as close as they both pretended to be. Their relationship was strained, both believing it was important to have a close brotherly relationship, but both not being able to achieve this. Connor suspected it was because of John's hard, harsh exterior. He had been sure there was more beneath the surface to John, but after being with him for as long as he had, he had come to the sad conclusion that John was who he appeared to be. There was no false mask for him, unlike Connor who wore a mask each day. It did occur to Connor perhaps the reason he and John weren't close was because of *him*. He had no doubt his whining and bitching about his marriage with Caroline took its toll on John, after all, who wants to hear some guy nagging all the time?

John looked at his baby brother sitting at the table they met once a week. His eyes narrowed at the tumbler of whiskey he held, wondering how much he'd had. His drinking had increased too much of late, so much so that John was beginning to worry. *Well*, he thought, *worry as much as I can when I'm screwing his wife.* Did he feel guilt about that? John titled his head thoughtfully as he neared the table.

"Hey John" his brother said with a cheery smile.

John lifted his eyebrow at Connor's smile and happy tone. His brother never greeted him in a happy mood; it was usually a depressing atmosphere.

"Connor" he replied with a nod, taking his place opposite. He signalled to the waiter to bring him the same as Connor, then sat back and contemplated his brother.

"So, why are you happy?" he finally asked. Connor looked up, a surprised expression crossing his face.

"No reason John, just feel happy. Life's good and all that"
"Yes, but you're life is never good and we both know it"
"Maybe Caroline's improved" Connor teased good naturedly, both knowing that would never be the cause of Connor's new found happiness. A small smile appeared on John's face, knowing personally Caroline hadn't spent her time with Connor recently. Just thinking about that woman got his blood pumping south, arousing him to no end. She certainly knew how to give pleasure, giving him the clean, detached relationship he desired. Well, he paid well for it, he reminded himself, but Caroline was worth the money. Looking at his younger brother now, he felt sorry for the man who hadn't enjoyed her touch for years. Again he wondered if he should feel guilty for having an affair with Connor's wife.
"Now, we both know that would never happen, Con, so come on, tell me"
"Are you really interested?"
John gave him a thoughtful look. Was he interested? Some part of him wished to know why Connor was happy, but he doubted it was for the right reasons. Perhaps he wanted to know because his interests laid with Caroline, and how much time she would be able to spare over the next week. He wouldn't begrudge Connor his happiness, but he wouldn't be distraught if his happiness disappeared overnight.
Nevertheless he answered "Of course"
Connor gave him a doubtful expression, knowing John was only being polite, but he took the chance to mention Scarlet, he needed to tell someone.

"Well, I met a woman" Connor would have laughed at the surprise on John's face, if it didn't make him so sad. Was it that surprising he could meet a new woman?
"I have to admit" John began while lighting a cigarette, inhaling and blowing the smoke away "I was not expecting that" he grinned, and took another drag.
Connor smiled in return thanking the waiter as he brought them another round of drinks. "Yeah, neither was I to be honest, John. Nothing's happened, you know, I wouldn't do that to Caroline"
"Why are you rushing to justify it? It isn't as if you and Caroline have a proper marriage"
Connor's smile fell from his lips at the reminder that his marriage was fake.
"Yeah, I am aware of that. But, I don't want you thinking I don't give a damn"
John flicked the ash off his cigarette. "I know you Con, I know you wouldn't do anything unless you were completely sure"
"Well nothing has happened" he said defensively "I just met her today and I don't know, she was fun…she made me smile"
"So, you met her in a club or…?"
"She's a new client of mine" Connor muttered
John laughed and took another drag, blowing smoke out as he said, "Oh Con, you know how to make it harder for yourself don't you? You know it's not smart to mix business with pleasure. Remember what happened with that Busty character?"
Connor shook his head, his eyebrow rising "You know, she mentioned that name too, why do I not know these things?"

"I don't know little bro, maybe because you've taken no interest in your career for the last...I don't know five years?"
Connor gave a sheepish smile "Yeah that might have something to do with it" he took a swig of his whiskey, liking the way it burned down his throat.
"So, you are going to ask her out?"
Connor shook his head, frowning "No, I don't think I'd go that far. It's just nice having someone making you smile again"
John regarded his brother and noticed the wistful look he had in his eye. It was obvious to him that Connor had been lonely, starved of intimacy for a long time. John wasn't one for intimacy himself, but then he preferred his relationships that way. But his brother was a man who craved intimacy, who wanted a relationship, someone to dedicate himself to. John shivered, he couldn't understand that desire.
"Yeah, well, that's good then" John suddenly felt awkward, not relating to Connor this way; he didn't like it when he spoke of sentimental topics.
Connor seemed to shrug himself out of a daydream, and then looked at John. "Anyway, how are you John? What have you been doing recently?"
John smiled, wanting to say, *your wife*, but knew he would never say it. It would ruin the easy life he had. He stubbed his cigarette out, and sat back, casually observing his brother as he chose how to answer.
"This and that, nothing special mate"
He was rewarded a laugh, and narrowed his eyes at Connor's amusement. "What?" he asked suspiciously.
Connor's eyes twinkled with humour "You're always doing something, John, I know you, and you can't resist an adventure"

John didn't like the way this conversation was going, well aware what Connor thought of his lifestyle. Strange how they were so different, but shared the same blood.
"So who's the woman who gave you this happy mood?"
Again that wistful look took place upon Connor's face. "Scarlet Windsor"
John sputtered on the whiskey he'd just taken, and promptly burst into a coughing fit, hardly being able to believe what he'd heard.
"S-s-scarlet Windsor?" he repeated
"Yeah, what's the problem John, you ok?"
Oh yes, he was more than ok. He killed the urge to laugh at Connor, knowing his brother wouldn't appreciate it. *Silly sod*, he thought, *trust Connor to take an interest in a woman who had her own past and secrets.* He lifted an eyebrow, wondering if it was fate that brought them together, God knows they suit each other. He quickly killed that notion, damn Connor for putting sentimental thoughts, such as fate, into his mind.
"Con, you do know who Scarlet Windsor is, right?"
It was Connor's turn to look suspicious. "Well, she's an actress, funny, she's down to earth-not a balloon head like my other clients"
"Yeah, yeah she's got a hot body, but do you know her reputation?"
"No"
"God, how long have you been out of the world of celebs?"
Connor looked defensive as he answered "Long enough to know I don't miss it. Now tell me, what about her reputation?"

John leant forward, looking in his brother's eyes, intent on making him listen to him. Connor may want to embark on an affair, but he chose the worse woman to do it with. Was it brotherly protectiveness he felt for Connor? Why else would he feel the need to warn him? No, maybe he just didn't like Connor being happy, some part of him resented the wistful happy look that crossed his face when he spoke of Scarlet. Oh, Lord, he wasn't…jealous was he? He didn't want a relationship, he despised intimacy, yet something inside of him responded to Connor's sentimental talk. This revelation horrified John, he must nip this in the bud right now, he will not succumb to this weakness, this need like Connor does. His father's word rang in his ears, his cruel constant claims that John was weak, that he was useless, before he'd take his belt out and proceed to punish John for these characteristics. Never once had Connor gotten the belt, or the harsh words, he had been the golden boy, he had been his father's favourite. The bitterness still lived in his heart, even though he'd managed to quench his desire for revenge. This was the real reason he and Connor could never be close, their upbringing had prevented John from feeling any softer emotions, while Connor was full of them.
So John was faced with a decision. He could make Scarlet's tedious celebrity past into something more, perhaps exaggerate on a few facts, to make Connor forget about any romantic notions he may have about her. Or, he could tell him the truth, about her sad abandonment, the heartless actions of a gypsy mother, and make him feel sympathy for the woman, perhaps leading him to feel more for her. Tricky decision.
"Do you want to fuck her?" John suddenly asked, needing to know the depth of Connor's feelings.

"Well… I …God I…" Connor looked embarrassed, swallowing thickly. His eyes narrowed, wondering why John would ask such a personal question, but if he knew his brother, which sometimes he doubted, he suspected John was trying to throw him off-balance. He'd always been the blunt one, wanting to shock people, wanting to make them vulnerable. Or maybe he just did it to him. Connor knew John thought him stupid because he liked a relationship instead of bed-hopping. But no, he decided, John wouldn't throw him off course.

"Yes, yes I do" If he was expecting to see surprise in John's expression, he was wrong. Nothing changed; he looked as if he could have been discussing the weather.

"Do you think she's hot?"

"Yes, incredibly hot"

"More so than Caroline?"

Connor narrowed his eyes, wondering why he'd ask such a question. "John, I haven't been with Caroline that way for years"

"So why think of having an affair, why not just pleasure yourself?"

Connor snorted "It's been so long, pleasuring myself has become tedious."

John smirked a little, and then his expression turned serious once again. "Why not hire a whore? They would do more than Scarlet would, and they wouldn't make you work for it."

"No, they'd make me pay for it instead"

Both brothers's stared at each other as silence settled round their table. They sized one another up, both contemplating how far the other was willing to go. Finally John broke the spell by swigging the last of his whiskey and leant forward, arms crossed on the table.

"Scarlet Windsor" he smiled a little "She's quite a woman. Has a so-so past. Nothing major. But as a celebrity, it always helps to be a little tortured right?" At Connor's nod of agreement, John continued "She comes from a gypsy family; they travelled from place to place, field to field, setting up home wherever they could. How do you think she came by that red hair and yet has incredibly tanned skin?"
"I don't know, I didn't think she had been a gypsy"
"Well, she has been. I know the conventional look for a gypsy is dark, black hair, but that's what made Scarlet stand out. Some of the other gypsy families didn't like her look; I heard that they thought she was a bad influence and that she made them memorable. No one would forget hair like hers would they?" Connor shook his head as John sighed. "So, her mother was pressured into deciding to leave the gypsy group, or leave her daughter. She chose to leave her daughter."
Connor's look of utter disgust made John smile again. "I know who would leave their child? The way she did it though-that's the worst part of the story. Scarlet was sent to school as usual then when she came home, or well, the field they called home, nothing was there. Only a pile of rubbish was left behind."
"What did she do after that?"
John took a breath, deciding to embellish this part of the tale. "Well what does a woman do who has nothing?" at his meaning, Connor's expression went to shock, then to anger, then to disbelief.
"But…she was just a child!"
"Well, she was sixteen, not so much a child in the eyes of men"
"Oh God, that's horrible!"

"Yeah, but what other choice did she have? I wouldn't judge her too harshly; you of all people should know what mother's force their children into."
At that comment, Connor's eyes glittered warningly, daring John to go into the subject he had avoided for the last six years.
"I don't want to talk about her" he said in a strained voice
John nodded, apparently letting the conversation end. For now. Connor sighed, thinking about Scarlet and how much she resembled what he wanted, a relationship, happiness, love. But now, after finding out about her past and what she had been forced to do, well, it was too close to his current situation to not be tainted by it. He wanted something completely fresh, completely new, and completely separate from the fake false life he was forced to live. He wanted something *real.*
"What did I do to deserve this life, John?" he said with a sigh.
There was only silence for a minute, then Connor looked up and saw John staring at him with such anger and bitterness, he felt the urge to shrink away for it. But as quickly as it had appeared, it was gone, leaving him to think he had imagined it.
"You married the wrong woman, Con, you married a woman who has her own dirty past, and what happened that night six years ago, well, you made a decision then and there to stick with her"
Suddenly anger boiled up within Connor, causing him to clench his fists atop of the table. "I didn't know what she was really like." He muttered through clenched teeth; spit forming between each gap, his chin taut with unsuppressed rage. "If I had known what a cold,

unfeeling bitch she really is, I would've let her suffer the consequences of her actions. God, she never told me the truth of her past, I had to find out that *night*" he spat out the word as if it were dirty "how she'd trapped me, and like a fool I took her reasoning. So I agreed to help her and keep silent about what she did. But oh God, how I regret that day, she's ruined my life, ruined my chance for any happiness." Silence once again settled between the two brothers, both unused to emotional outburst such as Connor's.

John kept silent, inwardly surprised by the emotion his brother had displayed. Connor never showed any emotion about that night, he didn't speak of it, but now John could see the rage he himself harboured and suddenly didn't resent his brother as much as he did. If anything, John felt a slight sympathy for the man. Because, living each day with anger was the one of the worst things a man could do. For anger made a lousy companion.

Susie

The old woman met the man in the darkest corner of the public house. Her eyes widened when she saw him pull out the wad of bank notes.

"Which one do ya want, lovie?" she asked, licking her lips as she regarded the cash.

"Someone who will suit my needs" the man replied. He looked at the old woman, taking in her badly applied lipstick, her yellow teeth and her salivating mouth as she looked at his money. Woman, he snorted, they were all the same. Show em the cash and they'll do anything for it. From spreading their legs to sucking his cock.

"What d'ya mean, "your needs"?"

He looked at her "Anything I want"

She chuckled "Feisty one are ya?" she asked with a wink.

"I need a woman who will do as she's told. When I want her to service me I expect her to without complaint. When I want her to cook me food, I expect her to prepare a banquet"

The old woman nodded, as if she got these requests everyday. "D'ya want a virgin or an experienced one?"

The man bit his lip, considering this. A virgin sure would be fun. He could rip through her barrier and pump her into her until she screamed from the pain. Oh Lord, just the thought of her screaming with pain made him hard. But no, he thought, he didn't want to break the girl, he needed to know she could handle a man between her thighs because he had many things he wanted to do with her.

"In between. Not a virgin but not some girl who needs to get tested. Ya know what I mean?" he looked

pointedly at the old woman, thinking she probably needed to be tested.
"I get ya, mister" she made a grab for the cash but he held it away from her.
"I wanna see the girl before"
"Sure thing, mister" the old woman said as she began walking to a door at the back of the public house. He followed her up the stairs and along a corridor with many doors . he wondered what delights lingered behind each door and felt himself begin to stir at the thought. He hoped his new girl would service him straight away.
"Here we are" the woman announced as she took a key out of her pocket and unlocked the door. The man peered in, his eyes searching for the girl. Then he saw her. Oh, how he saw her. She stood in the corner of the room, naked, expect for her high heel shoes. She looked like a goddess. Her brown hair hung around her shoulders and her slim body was illuminated from the small lamp in the corner of the room. The man's mouth went dry as he looked at her body. It was a slim body but muscular at the same time. Her breasts were high, her nipples erect. His gaze travelled down her body until he saw the patch of brown hair covering her pussy. He nearly came on the spot just thinking about what he could do with this body.
"So?" the old woman demanded, impatient and wanting the money he promised.
"Here" he said as he handed the cash to her, glancing back at the girl "She'll do nicely"
"Nice doing business with ya, mister." The woman began to walk away then turned back to the girl "Remember what I said, girl and then you'll be alright."
"What's her name?" the man questioned.

"Susie" the woman answered as she walked down the corridor and then disappeared from sight.
"Pack you things, Susie" the man said, looking at her with lust blazing in his eyes.
"Where am I going?" Susie asked quietly, wondering why this man hadn't pounced on her yet like all the other's did.
"You're going to be my wife, little girl, so chop chop, get your stuff and lets go get hitched"
"Married?" she shrieked.
The man's eyes narrowed "Something wrong with that?" he walked closer to her "Am I not good enough for a whore like you?"
"I…uh…no I wasn't-"
"I think you were" he suddenly grabbed her by the hair and yanked her head upwards so she looked him in the eye. "We're going to have a good life; you gotta do as I say, when I say it. If ya do, then there'll be no problem."
She nodded shakily "Yes, ok ok."
He seemed satisfied with her answer and released his hold on her hair. He pushed her away, causing her to stumble a few paces. His mocking laugh echoed in the dull, empty room. "Don't worry, ya don't need your balance to stand." He reached down and grabbed a hold of the bulge in his trousers "You'll be on your back most of the time anyway"
Her eyes widened as he touched himself while staring at her. No man had ever done that in front of her before. Men usually came in her room, mounted her for a few minutes and then left.
She asked the question she had been taught to ask every man "Do you want me to service you?" The question seemed to snap this man's self-control for her suddenly

strode towards her and pushed her roughly against the fall. She looked at him, fear in her young eyes and he turned her around and pulled her hips away from the wall.
“I’m gonna do you so hard up against this wall, then I want you to suck my cock” he mumbled as he unfastened his trousers. Susie closed her eyes tightly and felt a burst of pain as he forced himself into her, shoving her back forward so her cheek was crushed against the wall. Tears filled her eyes at the pain he was causing her and shock made her body tremble. No man had ever been this rough with her. Suddenly she felt his hands on her breasts, pinching hard, squeezing until she cried out. His laugh vibrated in her ears.
No! She silently screamed, *this is wrong, this is all wrong.*
The man shouted and stiffened, then collapsed on top of her. The weight was so heavy that Susie collapsed under it, falling to the floor with the man on top of her.
“What?” he roared, grabbing her harshly by the arm and yanking her. He sneered at her then pulled back and smacked her across the face. The pain exploded across her jaw and she fell down with the force of it.
“You let me fall to the ground with you? Do you have no respect for your future husband? Fuckin’ ungrateful whore.” He pulled his trousers up and looked at her “Come on then, get ya stuff. We’re off”
Susie looked up at the man who was going to be her husband. She held her jaw, aware of the blood starting to drip down onto the floor from her mouth. Susie looked at her hand, covered in her blood, vowing one day it would be his.

Chapter Three

She knocked on the hotel door; idly patting her wig, making certain her appearance was what he would require. Mr. Black telephone call had been rather mysterious, only giving her the name of the hotel and the number of the room. The door opened harshly, the air hitting her in the face as she looked up at the figure before her. At once desire swirled in her belly, hot warmth spread all the way down to her private place. She suppressed a giggle; she wondered what Mr. Black would ask her to call her "private place" tonight. His crude words had a way of turning her body to soft, yielding mess, ready for him and his demands.
"Caroline" he murmured, and all at once she knew something was wrong. He never called her by her name during their sessions.
"Mr…Back?" she said hesitantly
"No, not tonight. Tonight I'm John"
She looked uncomfortable, and then stepped into the room, taking her wig off and throwing it on the bed. She felt angry, angry at John for ruining their game. How she'd wanted to come and play one of their games! She turned slowly back to him, maintaining her composure, awaiting his explanation.
"I'm sorry if I gave you the wrong…impression about what tonight is about"
"Yes, you could say that" she replied, icily.
John started at her, noticing her stiff stance, her cold voice and realised what Connor had meant a few days ago when they had met up. When he'd referred to her as a "Cold, unfeeling bitch" John hadn't been so sure, considering how responsive he was when he was

fucking her. But then, he never spoke to her as Caroline when they were alone.

"I wanted to tell you something about Connor" at the mention of her husband, Caroline's eyes widen ever so slightly, but then returned back to normal.

"What about the man?"

"He has a new interest"

John had expected surprise, doubt but hadn't expected her to laugh so loudly.

"I am serious Caroline, Connor has hired a new actress, called Scarlet Windsor and he made it clear he might try something"

Her laughter died down, and the flat, emotionless look came into her eyes again. "Connor would never do anything like that, he has too many morals"

John lifted his eyebrow "If a man goes long enough without sex, his morals won't even save him. And from the sounds of it, you haven't exactly been near him"

Caroline gave him a mocking expression "Are you saying I should go to my husband's bed, John? I should let him touch me as you touch me? Or that I should touch myself, letting him know the way I like it?"

At the image of Caroline touching herself, John felt himself starting to swell in his trousers. "No, I didn't say that, but Connor is like any other man, he may have morals but in the long run his cock will get the better of him"

"So what? What do I care if he has sex with this Scarlet?"

John sighed as he looked around the room "Connor may fall in love with her"

"Good"

His gaze returned to her sharply. "Good? You little idiot, why would you say that? Do you realise if he falls

in love your secret with be endangered? He may leave you, and then your past will be out. What will happen then?"
From the fleeting expression of panic that crossed Caroline's face, she understood his meaning. She cleared her throat as he walked to the bed, where she sat and crossed her legs elegantly. *Always the lady*, he thought humourlessly.
"Well, what do you propose I should do about it?"
John loosened his tie as he made his way to the canter of whiskey. He offered it to Caroline and with a shake of her head, he began pouring.
"I think you should keep an eye on the situation. It wouldn't hurt to consider her a threat" at that Caroline snorted, but John carried on "I don't want your secret getting out, so you should treat this cautiously"
"Why do not want our secret getting out?"
He considered that answer, wondering how to answer that. He didn't know himself. He didn't want their secret getting out because it would ruin the situation they had together, just sex, nothing more complicated. But he had a feeling he wanted to protect Caroline from her secret from being revealed. Yes, he wasn't overly happy Connor might find happiness, which did have something to do with his decision, but he truly believed Caroline's past would be in danger if Connor fell for Scarlet.
But he couldn't let Caroline know the extent of her feelings, he didn't even want to acknowledge this feeling he was starting to experience, so he answered, "I want to continue our relationship, just sex, nothing more."
His answered seemed to satisfy her, as she got up from her seating position and strolled towards him.

"Well, then, Mr. Black, shall we resume our easy relationship?" the shift to his game name let him know what she expected.
"Yes, we shall"
He reached out and began to fondle her breast, even through the layers of her smart, casual jacket he could feel the nipple harden, he could sense her desire. Even if she was cold, even if she was heartless in some cases, whenever he touched her, she melted beneath him, she became a different woman. A passionate, alluring woman, who could seduce any man into caring for her. He took her jacket off and saw the white blouse she wore underneath. "Undress yourself, and then touch your pussy and tell me how wet you are" he turned his back to her, taking his own clothes off, and took the final gulp of his whiskey. How easily he slipped into the crude, lover role she desired in him. When he was naked he turned back around to her, seeing she had laid herself on the bed, as her fingers slid between her legs with expertise. He wondered how many men she'd done this for when she was a whore. Did they pay her extra? He shut his eyes at the questions, oh god, why was he suddenly curious? And why did he feel jealousy slam into his chest, making him angry at all those men who touched her, even his brother. He opened his eyes and watched her; she was looking at the ceiling, still using her fingers.
"How wet are you?" he asked with a rugged breath
She gasped at his words "I'm incredibly wet, just dripping for you Mr. Black, just waiting for you to fill me"
He started as a shaft of desire shot through him, settling on his bulging erection. Oh god, he was so hard, he just

wanted to pump in and out of her, with no mercy, until he came hard and fast in her wet welcoming pussy.

"You want to have my cock inside you?"

"Yes, oh God yes"

He strode over to her, and knelt next to her on the bed, removing her fingers and replacing them with his own.

"Do you like it when I touch you?"

She groaned in an answer. "Do you like my fingers right" he moved his index finger inside her, while his thumb started rubbing back and forth on her clit. "-here?"

"Oh, yes, please don't stop"

Did Connor touch her like this? Did he feel her clit beneath his thumb? Did he continue until she came over his fingers? He drove himself crazy with the constant questions that plagued his mind. Why did he keep asking himself these things?

Suddenly Caroline began to shudder and he stopped his actions, only to replace his fingers with his cock, and thrust deep inside of her, going hard and fast between her thighs, reassuring himself that she only thought of him when he gave her this pleasure. He lifted his body off of hers, still thrusting inside her, but be able to watch their joining down between their bodies. "Watch. Watch me take you" Caroline peered down at John's orders and saw his cock pumping into her with such force, she felt herself beginning to convulse. John noted Caroline was near her pleasure, and desperately wanting to join her there; he increased his pace, pounding into her with such ferocity, the bed banged against the wall. As her moans began, he felt the delicious pressure begin to build and plunged deeper inside her. He held himself there as he joined her in ecstasy, feeling his seed leave his body, groaning in satisfaction. He rolled off Caroline and laid next to her as he got his breath back. He enjoyed these times with Caroline, but he just hoped Connor wasn't going to ruin it all.

"No, that idea is insane" Scarlet proclaimed as she regarded Busty.
"Why? What's so crazy about it? Tons of actress's have parties, plus this one would work in your favour 'cos you have the hot Mr Belle in your corner" she said with a wink.
Scarlet winkled her nose; she knew she shouldn't have told Busty about Connor-Mr. Belle's- good looks. Busty would hold it over her for a long time to come. But, oh Lord, Scarlet did think that man attractive. Shame about his choice of career, but there seemed to be more to Mr Belle than he let on. She was intrigued; she had to admit that, but intrigued enough to act on it? She still wasn't sure. Not to mentioned his very real, very present marriage to Caroline Belle. Scarlet wasn't a woman to get involved with a married man; she knew the pain caused by being betrayed. Her mother had betrayed her when she made the decision to leave her, and she swore she'd never inflict that pain on anyone. Although Scarlet didn't want to admit it, Busty's idea did make sense. It would put her in the spotlight; allow her to build bridges for her scarred reputation. Because as much as Scarlet hated the press, they were what made her career and, as Busty had said, she needed to "suck" up to them as much. The idea made her sick, but she would have to do it if she wanted to act. And God knew she wanted to act.
"I guess so" she murmered, deep in thought

Busty raised her eyebrows "You "guess so" about what? That Connor is hot or about the party?"
Scarlet frowned "The party of course"
"Of course" Busty echoed, slightly mockingly.
"Perhaps we should arrange it for about a month's time?"
"Hmm, I guess so; I'd do it sooner personally"
"Why?" she asked.
Busty studied her nails as she answered "Well, you need to get your career back on track asap, Hun, and who knows what's going to happen in a month?"
"What could happen? I'll just carry on as normal"
"Yeah," She leant forward, looking at Scarlet earnestly "but what if you and Connor get it on?"
Scarlet narrowed her eyes at her friend-did she seriously believe her to be able of having an affair with a married man? "He's married" she said flatly.
"Mean's nothing these days"
"Yes it does, it does to me anyway" she shrugged "I believe in it, I believe it's forever"
Busty snorted "Oh, come on Scar, I know you're a romantic and all, but love and marriage and forever don't exists anymore"
"When did you become so cynical?" Scarlet crossed her arms over her stomach as she sat back "You used to believe"
Busty looked away sharply, evidently finding the wall more appealing. "Yeah, well I was young then" Scarlet refrained from mentioning it was only three years ago, because Busty suddenly looked so small and scared. She changed the subject, aware of the feeling too well.
"So this party…" she ventured "Who would we invite?"

Busty seemed to snap herself out of her mood and smiled “Hmm…I’m not sure, we need to invite the big names…about two hundred people in total”
Scarlet chocked on her water “Wh.-what? Two *hundred*? “
Busty rolled her eyes “Oh, jeeze girl, come on, I know you don’t go out and even though you’re a celebrity, who is supposed to be all glam and parties, you don’t know much about these gatherings do you?”
She smiled sheepishly at Busty “No, and I know I should but ugh, it’s seems so fake”
“Yeah, well, we live in the world of fake, come on most of the people we meet are fake, their worries are about makeup and putting on a pound in weight”
“Then why are we in this world, Bust?”
Busty sighed as she looked at Scarlet, “Fuck knows.”
They both smiled and thought for a minute, Busty about the party and Scarlet about their careers. If they hated it so much, why did they do it? Scarlet suspected it was to do with the fact that they didn’t know anything else. Becoming an actress had been Scarlet’s only option all those years ago, but Busty did have a choice, and she realised they’d never discussed why she chose this life.
“Look, I’d talk to Connor-oh sorry-Mr Belle” she added at Scarlet’s look of warning “about this. He’s bound to come up with more ideas”
“Hmm, this is true. Although, when it comes to celebrities and PR he seems just as clueless as me”
“Well, sounds like you’re well suited then” busty said with a grin, enjoying teasing Scarlet about her crush.
“Busty! I have to say though-I wonder how he became so…established if he acts like he doesn’t even want my business?”

Busty tapped her mouth as she contemplated this "I heard he was incredible, I mean his skills and knowledge beat every other PR agent about six years ago. He made most of the names we know now; I mean he really knew his stuff. But, I guess he kind of just faded away after a few years, people do you know"
"Yeah, I get that, but he hasn't faded out, he's still there taking clients on, people are still going after him"
"Well, around six years ago, that's when his wife lost their baby, so maybe he decided to take a step back from it all."
Scarlet nodded, seeing sense in that "Yes, I couldn't blame him"
"Hmm, although Caroline seemed to flourish at that time, she came out of her shell."
Scarlet frowned as she said "Maybe she was trying to cover her pain"
Busty laughed humourlessly "Oh, come on, you'll meet her and see what I mean, her eyes….are just flat"
"I'm not getting into this conversation with you again Bust" Scarlet warned, rising from her sofa and walking to the kitchen "Remember we don't know what effect that had on her" she shouted behind her.
"Yeah, yeah I know, but it ain't right, Scar, that's all I'm saying"
"Shall we invite her to the party, do you think?" Scarlet asked as she returned to the lounge.
"Hmm, we have to really, she is Connor's wife"
"Yes, well, I think it'll be nice to meet her." Scarlet said, reassuringly, not sure if she was trying to convince herself.
"Yeah, it'll be nice" Busty said with a doubtful expression.

Connor had dressed as any other PR agent would. Yes, he had dressed smartly, merely because it was what he should do. It had nothing to do with any appointments or meetings he had today. It certainly had nothing to do with his afternoon meeting.

He hadn't relished the task of looking into the mirror at himself .In fact, he tried to avoid looking at himself as often as he could. Whenever he looked into his own eyes, he saw his own desperation and sadness, and it sickened him to think he felt this way because of his own doing. It would be so easy to blame Caroline for everything, but he knew he couldn't. He knew he could've made a different decision six years ago. It's a shame he hadn't known how much that one decision would shape the rest of his life. He shook his head, enough of thinking about Caroline; he had a job to do. Scarlet had faxed her idea of a party over to him yesterday, and he thought it a good idea. Not that he knew much about parties, but he hoped Pam, his receptionist would help him with that.

"Hey Pam, can you do me a favour?"

She disconnected from her head piece and took it off

"Sure, for you Connor, anything"

"You flatter me, Darling, but look I need a list of possible…entertainment"

"What sort of entertainment?"

"Well, um…"

Pam started up at him expectantly.

"Oh, balls to it; ok I need your help. Scarlet, uh, Miss Windsor wants to organise a party to get her career back on track, and you know what celebrities are like-"

"Give them free beer and a place to shag and they'll be your best mate" Pam interrupted bitterly. Connor abruptly stopped talking to look at his receptionist.

She's always been so helpful, but it occurred to him he didn't know much about her.
"Do you not like celebrities, Pam?" he ventured
She looked surprised "What makes you ask that?"
He smiled kindly at her "Well, it may have something to do with your tone when you speak of them, and how that particular tone could skin a donkey"
She frowned at his analogy, thinking it was odd. He pressed his lips together, knowing he should try to be witty, it didn't suit him and he ended making himself look a fool.
"Well, I don't like them; they're rude, arrogant and annoying"
"Then, may I ask why are you in this type of job?"
She shrugged "It pays well." She then titled her head thoughtfully "Why are *you* in this type of job?"
Because I have no choice. Connor's smile was strained as he considered this. He couldn't possibly tell Pam anything about his life, so instead, he did what he always did when faced with a question he didn't want to answer; he lied.
"Well, this job is better than most, I don't do much and get paid a fortune" He knew he sounded as shallow as most of the other PR agents did, but it was the only way.
Pam seemed to accept this answer, and he continued his reason for speaking to her.
"Well, anyway, Miss Windsor wants to organise a party and I was thinking of any new bands, or new acts that are around, someone who will benefit from the publicity, but also be fresh and new for all of the guests"
Pam nodded thoughtfully, making notes as Connor spoke. "I do know a duo actually"

"Yeah?"
"Hmm, they say they're the next Lennon and McCartney"
Connor raised his eyebrow, that was some compliment to be given, *especially in this tough world of critics and crap music*, he thought cynically.
"Do you think they'd be up for it?"
Pam looked at him with pity in her eyes "Connor, I'm sure they'd leap at the chance to perform where music labels, PR agents, and *women* are attending."
Connor suddenly felt old. He should've realised that on his own not rely on his twenty-six year old assistant to tell him.
"Ok, well give them a call" he started to walk away
"Connor, do you want to know what they're called, so you can tell Miss Windsor?"
"Sure" he answered turning back; again thinking he should've asked that before.
"Well, they don't really have a group name; they're just called by their own names"
"Hmm, seems fine to me, let me write them down" he said as he took a notepad and pen.
"It's James Owen and Ben Anthony"
As he wrote these names down he considered what it would be like to be these two young lads. Trying to make their way in the world with their music, and he wondered, were they trying for the right reasons? Life was so tedious that he hoped they wouldn't look back and regret. Oh, Lord, he thought as he thanked Pam and made his way to his office, he really was getting old.

Scarlet smoothed her skirt down as he rode the elevator up to level 5. She resisted the urge to look in her little

compact mirror for the tenth time. This was ridiculous! She didn't need to impress anyone, let alone her shallow, arrogant PR agent. She sighed, oh but he was so much more than that, she was certain. She wanted to deny how much Connor-Mr Belle- had been on her mind lately. They'd only had one conversation for heaven's sake! How much could you really tell about a person after one conversation?
The doors pinged open and Scarlet stepped out, her eyes scanning the reception area with little interest. She only had one door she needed to search for, and when she found it, she walked, confidently up to it. If only she felt confident on the inside!
"Oh, Miss Windsor?" a voice said behind her. Scarlet turned to see Connor's receptionist staring at her with a bright, happy smile.
"Yes?"
"If you'd just like to wait here, I'll inform Mr Belle you've arrived"
"Oh" Scarlet answered dumbly "Oh, yes of course" she turned to the seats, resisting the urge to slap herself on the forehead. How did she not remember to speak to his receptionist first? Why did she just stride up to his door? Thank Goodness she was stopped before she opened it by herself. She shook her head, all these nerves would just not do! She would not forget that what she and Connor, no, Mr Belle, shared was purely professional. The sooner she got her fluttering stomach to realise that, the better.

He looked better, Scarlet thought as she studied Connor from across the desk. He had shaved and chosen a neatly pressed dark suit, one that emphasised his blue eyes. Oh, how she could stare into those blue eyes all day! He smiled at her, a genuine smile which held warmth and pleasure. Could that pleasure be because she was here? she wondered, her heart beating slightly faster at the possibility. She was surprised at the change she sensed in him, the arrogance and self-confidence weren't present this time, only a man who seemed happy and…free. Free of any burden's he had.

"So, Scarlet, how have you been?" he asked.

"Not too bad, the usual" she smiled not sure what to answer to a question. She couldn't possibly tell the truth; that she'd been thinking about him!

"Usual? Do tell me what the "usual" is for Miss Scarlet Windsor?" There was a mocking glint in his eyes making them sparkle, memorising Scarlet, so that she just started dumbly into them.

"Oh" she suddenly exclaimed, embarrassed to be caught staring admiringly at him. He must know she admired him-she made it obvious enough!

"The usual?" she cleared her throat "oh, you know, partying…drinking…."

"Casual sex?" he interjected, his eyes going flat all of a sudden.

She swallowed past the lump in her throat "What makes you say that?"

He gave her one of his arrogant smiles, the one she hated. "Isn't that the way of life for a celebrity?"

She frowned; annoyed he would consider her a stereotypical celebrity. Even though she had said she's been partying and drinking, which of course, she had done no such thing.

"I'm surprised you would lump me into one category" she sniffed, looking offended.

He spread his hands defensively "Isn't that what you do to me?"

Yes, she thought, *I walked right into that one*. She had mis-judged him and she knew she should apologise, but for some irrational reason, she was hurt that he thought her one of the air-headed women who were out there. She had sensed there was more to him almost immediately, yet he seemed to just think her one type of person.

It miffed her to say the least.

"Well, yes I admit I did mis-judge you, at the beginning, and I had started to change my opinion about you" she licked her suddenly dry lips "until now of course"

He snorted "What have I done now? You've been in my office for oh," he looked at his watch "all of five minutes and I've offended you"

"Yes, you have. You assume I'm the type of girl to have sex with any man, and drink until I black out"

They stared at each other. Connor looked very confused as he scratched his jaw. She could see him trying to go over their conversation, looking for anything he might've said to cause this reaction from her. She knew she was out of order, but this man just got under her skin!

"I believe you said you went out partying and drinking"

She lifted her chin a fraction higher "Yes, well I don't"

Connor frowned "Then why did you say you did?"

She shrugged "I had nothing else to say to your question"

"Which was?"

"What the "usual" was for me"

He leaned forward, staring intently into her eyes. Again she was amazed at how clear his eyes were. She could safely assume many women had had the same thought.

A stab of jealousy surprised her, oh Lord, she wasn't going to start getting jealous was she?
"I'm sorry if I gave you the wrong impression. I don't think you a drunk or someone who has sex-" at that word, a little shiver ran down Scarlet's spine "-with men willy nilly." He smiled that genuine smile again, the one that spread to his cheekbones and showed his brilliantly straight teeth "Why don't we start again?"
"Yes" she murmured
"How have you been, Miss Windsor?"
She noted the change back to her surname and was surprised to feel disappointment.
"I've been great, thank you, how have you been?"
"Oh, you know, the usual" he said, grinning from ear to ear, clearing enjoyed tormenting her. She had no chance not to respond to his grin; it was infectious. She let herself laugh and was pleased when Connor joined her.
"I have to apologise, it's been a…stressful few days"
He leant back in his chair, nodding in agreement. "Tell me, Scarlet, why did you leave your last PR firm?"
She shifted in her chair "Well...Charlie-"
"Charlie?" he asked with a frown
"Yes, Charles Edwards, my last PR agent"
"Oh, right, I think I've heard of him-was he any good?" was there a hint of competitiveness in Connor's tone? No she must be imaging it, why would Connor want to prove himself better than Charles?
"He was ok. Until he decided my past was too much for him to handle" she added bitterly.
"He just dumped you?"
She nodded; aware he'd used the same word as she when she told Busty "Yeah, no warning, no nothing.

And the weasel thought I'd told people of my past because I was doing a publicity stunt!"
"That's ridiculous. If I were you, I'd dispute the fact that he just decided to stop representing you"
She shook her head "No, I know I could have, but I'm too tired of it. Plus, he was ok, but he was a weasel"
Connor rubbed his hand over his face, as if he was preparing himself for something.
"I'm sorry Scarlet, but I have to ask"
She held up a hand, stopping him mid-sentence "It's ok; I'm willing to tell you. After all, it is your right to know if you're going to represent me"
He chuckled "Nice to have a client who is willing"
"Yes, I can imagine the high maintenance, air heads you have to deal with"
Connor smiled at Scarlet, looking into her eyes sincerely "Yeah, it's nice to deal with a real woman"
Scarlet tried not to bask in his compliment, but a little thrill flipped in her stomach, making her acutely aware of herself as a woman. If she didn't stop this she'd start patting her hair self-consciously!
"Well, my past…it's a tricky situation to describe to be perfectly honest. Where do I start?" she asked, almost to herself
"Start where you feel most comfortable" he suggested, his eyes never leaving her face. She knew there was an intense attraction between them now, thankful it hadn't been one-sided. She saw how his eyes darkened each time she licked her lips, and how they followed her every movement. She could safely assume her eyes reflected his, for she'd never experienced this sharp desire before and was at a loss on how to deal with it. But she should give him an honest answer about her past, he did have a right to know and yet she found

herself wanting to tell him about it, she wanted to share her secrets with this man. Which was surely crazy! She hardly knew him!

"When I was young, me and Mama would travel a lot, I didn't mind, I used to see a lot of things and meet new people. Thing is, we would travel in a group with other families like us" she smiled wistfully "it was nice because I never was lonely even when Mama went off for a few days I had the other girls to play with" Scarlet glanced down at her clasped hands, her smile dying "But, it wasn't until I was older that I realised what we were, that people had a name for me and Mama and the other families" she looked up into Connor's eyes, "We were known as Gypsy's. I still didn't understand what that meant, and thought nothing of it, in fact I don't think I thought about it at all, I was young and carefree." She snorted "Naive more like." Scarlet sighed as she remembered those days of playing with dolls and taking part in games such as Hide and Seek. "Mama wasn't a happy lady. She could never settle down in one place with one job or one man. You say celebrities have sex with loads of people, my mum would have given them a run for their money." Scarlet smiled bitterly "I used to hear her. With them. Two at a time sometimes. I just didn't understand it at my young age. And even when I started growing up and realising what she was doing, I just didn't think about it. Who wants to think about their Mama's having sex with men?" Scarlet got up and walked towards the window, gazing out at the view of buildings "One day, I was sixteen, I went to school as I usually did. Nothing special happened that day, I did my lessons, I skipped lunch, and I played on my own by the oak tree. Finally the day was over, and I walked back to the field we were living in at that time. I remember that as I neared it, I stopped because I felt uneasy. I knew something was right, I just knew it" Tears formed in her eyes as she recalled that sad day, as a teenage girl being left by the one person she relied on the most. "So I broke out in a run, suddenly desperately eager to get back to my Mama so she could reassure me that I was being silly. But the field was clear. There was a pile of rubbish that they'd left behind, but I hardly noticed that as I stared at the space where my Mama had been." Her voice shook as she remembered falling to her knees, sobbing loudly as she tried to understand why her Mama had left her. "She had left me. Just cleared up and gone. I couldn't believe it, I didn't understand. I wondered if I'd done something wrong, but I'd always been well behaved, I didn't want to be a problem to anyone." Her lips rose in a self-mocking smile "Never did me any good though did it? I did everything to help everyone and I still got left behind"

"What happened then?" Connor's soft voice asked. She turned around to him, seeing the sympathy in his eyes, and noting there was no pity. She was glad; the last thing she wanted to see from Connor was pity. She turned towards him, returning to her seat, crossing her arms.

"There wasn't much I could do. I stayed in the field for another night, thinking she might feel guilt and come back. But I realised that wasn't going happen any time soon, I never gave up hope, I knew I had to find myself somewhere to go, something to eat and try to get some money."

Connor smiled as he nodded, as if he admired her sense. She chewed her lower lip, liking the way Connor's eyes followed the action. She suppressed a smile and continued her story. "I went to a shelter to start with, the women there were very nice, welcoming you know? They just let me know it was all ok. I stayed there for a while, but then the time came where I just had to leave, I don't know why I wanted to, but I just woke up one day and knew it was time" she smiled a little as she looked at Connor "Some would say I was silly for leaving, I had everything free, shelter, food, warmth. But, I just didn't like taking it all, giving nothing back." Her smile faded and she once again rose from her chair to stand by his desk. Her arms still wrapped around her mid-section. "So I got a job, nothing special, but as a cleaner in a bar, the pay was crap but it was better than nothing. The barman was a kind man he offered me the spare room above the pub, he took money out of my wages for the rent, even thought it wasn't nearly enough to afford the room. I suppose he was lonely as his own wife had died and his children had left home. I was very fortunate to have met him. He never took advantage of me in anyway for which I will always be thankful. Eddie was his name" Scarlet sighed softly "I like to think I helped him as well, giving him company, making him laugh, allowing him to enjoy his life."

"What happened to him?" Scarlet looked at Connor, sadness showing in her eyes.

"He died. He had a heart attack when he was away visiting his children. He left me in charge of the bar; I was nearly twenty then so I was capable, and I got a call from his daughter saying Eddie had died. I couldn't believe it, but then, things did have a way of surprising me." She smiled softly as she recalled Eddie and his kindness. She then sighed as she thought about how he was taken from her as well. "His children wanted to sell the pub, neither had any use for it anymore, so I helped them, what else could I do? After Eddie had helped me the least I could do was help his children. His daughter, called Sarah, insisted I become her assistant. She was a theatre manager, a small new theatre in London, and needed people she could trust. She claimed she could trust me because her father had, and she said it was what Eddie would've wanted. I suppose as it was a new theatre, I didn't need extensive experience; I learnt on the job. I was happy in that job, that's how I came to know about the acting world and the plays, you see I'd never had the education to learn about Shakespeare or Keats or anything related to literature. I was so interested in that world, I became obsessed. Quiz me on any Shakespeare play; I know I'll beat you" she smiled at Connor "As the theatre grew and received a reputation, my duties became bigger, like organising the cast and crew, helping with the stage settings, a little bit of this and that really. I even played as an extra once in Shakespeare's *Twelfth Night* I was so nervous! But I did it, and I had such a great adrenaline rush that I was addicted from that night on. The manager of the production company noticed me as well. He then approach me offering me a small position as an extra in his company, again the pay was minimal but I loved it passionately. Sarah was sad to see me go, but she had noticed my zest for acting as well, so she sent me with her best wishes" Scarlet looked away from Connor, studying her finger nails. "My life was pretty good considering, but it went downhill when I joined Peter's production group" she grew quiet as she remembered Peter always letting her know how to make extra money. Her skin still crawled when she thought of his disgusting leer, his clammy hands trying to steal a feel when she passed him backstage.

"What did he do?"

Scarlet's eyes snapped back to Connor, aware of how much she'd revealed to him, how many personal details that he needn't know. He didn't need to know about Eddie or Sarah and he certainly didn't need to know about Peter.

"I think I've said enough for one day" she murmured, willing him to accept it.

Connor looked as if he might argue, but something seemed to have stopped him. Maybe it was the silent plea in her eyes, he wasn't sure. Perhaps it was because she looked so God damn beautiful sitting on the edge of his desk, her eyes raw with emotion. He knew the type of person she was now, and he relieved to discover she bore no resemblance to Caroline. She hadn't told him about the prostitution part of her past, but he suspected she was getting to it. Did it bother him? Yes, a little perhaps but then who was he to judge her? She had been left by her own mother to fend for herself, and she clearly didn't feel proud or comfortable when talking about it. Would he let that stop him from seeing Scarlet as the gorgeous, courageous, talented woman she was now? He frowned as he thought about it. Caroline had spoken proudly, happily about her past conquests and adventures with other men to him when he had found out. She had felt no shame, and it set his teeth on edge when he remembered how she'd delivered the news. No, Scarlet was, thankfully, nothing like Caroline, and he wished he could act upon this desire and admiration he felt for her.

"Of course, it's your decision. Well" he said as he sat back "I don't see how there's any reason the press

shouldn't know about this" at her look of panic he added "I mean the parts you want them to hear. We can confirm the rumour that your mother left you, and that you got a job in a theatre, but we wouldn't mention anything else." He paused and tapped his chin thoughtfully "Unless you wanted to?"
She shook her head "No, the less they know the better as far as I'm concerned."
He nodded in agreement, standing up to walk towards her. "Ok, well I'll make a statement for you, and I'll also mention your upcoming party and that we'll distribute invites as soon as possible."
She smiled "I suspect everyone will be my best friend when they hear about the party"
"Yes, celebrities are somewhat…fickle"
Scarlet started up at him as he stood before her. She swallowed as she asked her next question "Am I right in assuming you don't consider me one of these celebrities anymore?"
Connor didn't smile as she expected, instead he looked down at her with such dark intensity, and it took her breath away. She read the need in his eyes and recognised it easily as she felt it herself. The need for intimacy, for love, and more presently, the need to touch one another. Perhaps she should kiss him, she thought, her gaze travelling over his firm lips. Just one light touch would quench this urge, she was sure of it!
"I never thought you were" he whispered gently, briefly bringing her mind back to the question she had asked. His eyes looked all over her face, she felt his gaze as it burnt her, leaving a fiery trail in its path. It touched her chin, her lips, her cheeks and rested on her eyes. She gasped at the stark desire burning brightly in his blue gaze.

"Your eyes are so very beautiful" she said, barely louder than a whisper. He didn't answer her, but lifted a hand to touch her cheek softly; he ran a finger down to her chin, falling away gently. It was almost as if the touch had never happened and she felt a sharp pang of disappointment run through her body as he stepped back, breaking the intense spell they had woven of desire and need.

"I-" Connor cleared his throat as his voice broke "Um, I will notify you of when I have given the statement."

"Yes…I…" Scarlet was at a loss for words, and she stared at him dumbstruck at what to do. She gathered her wits, knowing she needed to get out of there "Yes, thank you. I should go now" she added hastily, picking up her bag and all but running to the door.

"Scarlet" his voice stopped her. She stood where she was, and looked over her shoulder at him, standing at the edge of his desk, looking as puzzled as her. She waited for him to speak, but when he said nothing and only stared at her with bewilderment. She gave him a shaky smile and fled the room.

Susie

"Suck it harder, bitch" The man said as he grabbed her hair. "Yeah, like that, bitch"
The name "bitch" seemed to be his favourite of the week. Susie knew it would change though; he had enjoyed calling her numerous names in the last year of their marriage. Suddenly he grabbed her head and forced his cock down her throat, she gagged as a reflex motion, but he didn't notice as he reached orgasm, his seed shooting down her throat. He threw her away roughly, buttoning his trousers as he walked away and up the stairs in their small, grotty cottage. When Toby had showed her where they were going to live, Susie had pretended excitement as she feared receiving a beating. The cottage they lived in was run down and falling to pieces. She was quite sure it had been abandoned and was just left to rot, but she didn't dare voice her thoughts.
To her dismay, Toby had meant what he had said that day in her room. He had ordered her to the small chapel in her town and ordered the priest to perform the ceremony. The priest had refused at first, looking worriedly at Susie's darkening chin and had stood firm. Well for all of five minutes. Toby had proceeded to take out a knife and had laid it calmly on the bench beside him. He then had taken another thick roll of money and placed it on the bench, beside the knife.
"It's you choice, preacher man" he had said, while he'd held Susie roughly by the elbow.
Needless to say the priest had preferred the cash.
So, from then onwards Susie had turned into Susie Shore, wife of Toby Shore, victim of rape and beatings. At first Susie had remained quiet, doing what was

asked of her which normally was service him when he was horny and cook him food when he was hungry. Toby had seemed pleased with her and hadn't beaten her for the first three months of their marriage. Susie had hoped it had been a one time thing and that she had been rude and needed to be taught a lesson. She had even gone as far as to imagine that the marriage could turn into a loving relationship. Perhaps not love, but they could care and respect for one another.

How wrong she was.

One day Toby came home in a stinking mood. Susie had learnt to remain quiet when he was in these types of moods and had carried on with cooking his dinner. She placed his meal, which consisted of scrambled eggs and bacon with some toast, on the table and awaited his arrival at the dinner table. It had been fifteen minutes when Toby hadn't come downstairs for dinner and she didn't dare shout up to him, as he didn't like it when she raised her voice to him. She decided to walk upstairs and see if he was alright. It was quiet when she reached upstairs and took a tentative step forward to the open bathroom door. She peered inside, noting nothing seemed out of the ordinary. The only other room in their cottage was the main bedroom and surprisingly the door was closed. She swallowed nervously before pushing it open (as they didn't have door handles) and looking for her husband. Then that's when she saw him. He standing over a magazine, touching himself the way he did on the day they first met. The chords in his neck stood out and his teeth were clenched as he pumped his hand up and down his cock. Susie followed his hand movements, her gaze going from his tightly shut eyes to his moving hand. She was unsure what to do, but decided it was best to leave. Sadly, Toby chose

that moment to open his eyes and look directly at his wife. He stopped moving his hand, his erection going soft and the magazine dropping from his hand.
"What the fuck do you think you are doing?" he demanded. Susie opened her mouth to tell him about his dinner, but no words came out. He looked down at his deflated penis then to his wife. She gasped at the rage she saw in his eyes. Without thinking, she turned and began to run away from him. He roared, and lunged for her, catching her within three strides. He lifted her from the waist and threw her violently against the wall. She banged against it and slid to the floor in a lump.
"You fuckin' whore. Ruining my fuckin' climax. You're gonna pay, bitch,"
He strode over and lifted her up, locking her against the wall with one arms across her chest. With his right hand, he clench his fist and punched Susie in the face. Her head banged against the wall with the force of it, and her tooth dropped out of her mouth.
"You're paying no, bitch, you think you can control me" he punched her again "Well you can't. You do as I tell ya to" he grabbed her chin, forcing her swelling eyes to look at him. He laughed cruelly, squeezing the bruise marring her chin, "You're a pathetic bitch. I dunno why I ever married ya" he then reared back and punched her in the ribs, causing her to scream out in pain. "Yeah, scream, you know what that does to me" his hand fondled his growing erection. Again he laughed at her, dropping his arms, letting her fall to the floor with a hard thump. Susie couldn't see out of her eyes, she could only feel the constant pain holding her head captive. She tried to lift a hand to her aching ribs but Toby kicked her hand away. She didn't have the strength to try and fight him, she just felt so very tired.

So when Toby took his penis out and started masturbating over her lifeless form, all she did was renew the vow that she would see his blood instead of hers.

Chapter four

Connor sat in his study, holding the familiar tumbler of whiskey in his hand. *At least I know what to expect of whiskey,* he thought, peering into the glass. There would be that blazing trail of fire moving smoothly down his throat, where it would ooze and settle in his stomach, instantly having that ever needed calming effect. Only, in this instance, Connor was drinking to numb the fierce, savage ache that had held his body hostage this past week, more precisely, these past five days in which he'd spent in close proximity of a certain actress with flaming red hair and a seductress smile. Damn her! Damn her for being gorgeous and alluring and sexy and everything Connor wanted but couldn't have. Because he couldn't, he knew it, so why did he keep imagining her in his bed, naked and welcoming? "I must hate myself" he mumbled, sighing as he settled the glass down. He wasn't sure if he was torturing himself because he believed he should be punished for what happened six years ago, or if he was just a plain idiot, drooling and fantasying over what he can't have. "I hate that word" he said aloud, his voice echoing silently in the silence of the room. What puzzled him was that Scarlet seemed to be feeling the same demanding desire as he was. Which, quite frankly astounded him. He had never considered himself an ugly man, but neither had he thought himself overly attractive, but Scarlet's eyes spoke of her sexual awareness of him; how they widened when he was close by, how they watched him when she thought he wasn't looking. Oh yes, there was definite sexual tension between them, and they were both aware of it, so why couldn't it be that simple? Connor chuckled at his train of thoughts “Because things are never simple” he got up and walked to his window, looking out into the darkness. He had only one option, which was to ignore whatever he felt for Scarlet. It would complicate his life more so than it already was if he didn’t, and lord knows he didn’t need anymore complications. He’d just act coldly to her, answer her questions with a nod or shake of the head; he would not laugh at her jokes, or smile at her, or stare at her mouth, imagining all the wicked, wonderful things she could do with it….No! “Enough!”

He shut his eyes as if to block out her image, but she was forever there taunting him.

Connor swallowed, and set his shoulders straight. He could do this! He was Connor Belle, master of appearances and facades; he could pretend he wasn’t interested in Scarlet Windsor.

Couldn’t he?

“You got it bad girl” Busty declared, looking at Scarlet’s reflection in the mirror. She wore a black satin, knee length dress, that dipped in at her tiny waist and hugged the flare of her hips. Her luxurious red hair was swept to hang over one shoulder, but she had left it loose so that it hung at its full length, which was to the middle of her back.

Scarlet no longer denied it to her friend, she was past the pretending now; she wanted Connor Belle with a need that was exhilarating as it was frightening.

“He’s married” she replied lamely.

“Doesn’t mean he’s not hot”

“He is hot, but that’s not the point. Sure I want to kiss him, have him grab me, bite my ears and suck on my-”

"Woah!" Busty interrupted, "I know you only have me as a mate but jeeze, I don't want to know every detail." Her eyes twinkled as she looked at Scarlet, "however, telling Mr Belle these thoughts may get you what you want."

Scarlet shook her head. She could never tell Connor for she knew he was a man who wouldn't betray his wife, and as far as she was concerned, he was happy in his marriage.

"He's married, probably very happily with Caroline, why would he risk that for me? Besides" she continued with a shrug "I wouldn't want a man who I knew was capable of cheating"

Busty rolled her eyes and clucked her tongue "So many couples have broken up over affairs and they go on to have committed relationships. Look at Bradd Pitt and that Angelia woman, they're all loved up and commited"

"Yeah but we don't know if they had an affair beforehand"

"God, Scar, you really need to look at the world with a realistic eye. Of course they did! He wouldn't give up a woman like Jenifer Aniston if he didn't know Angela was good in the sack"

Scarlet shook her head and walked away from the mirror "Sometimes Bust, you really need to dilute your sentences"

"I just tell it like it is"

"Sometimes people don't want to hear it"

"Ok Scarlet" she said as she followed her into the lounge and sat beside her "But I will say this to you. You look really hot tonight, and all this for a meeting with Connor. A meeting he suggested you guys have out of office hours so he could pay attention to your

party. The way I see it" she took Scarlet's hand and rubbed it gently "This man wants you, wife or not, so you need to prepare yourself for it"
"But I couldn't do it. I mean I know I want him, but knowing he was cheating on someone, breaking her heart like…" her words trailed off as she guiltily looked at Busty.
"Like me" Busty finished for her. Her friend got up and hugged her arms around her waist. "Scarlet, I was heartbroken, you know that but I wouldn't have given up what I had with him…" Busty stopped speaking and looked outside the window, her back facing Scarlet. If Scarlet could have seen Busty's expression, she would've seen her eyes fill with tears as the memories of the time where her and her lover had been happy. Where Busty had felt so complete, her heart could have burst with love. That time was the only time she had ever felt as if she belonged, as if she had a purpose. Then he ruined it. He tore her heart out and fed it to a pack of hungry wolves, and they had feasted on her emotions, and ripped the word "love" from her, for she would never allow herself to feel that for a man again. But, she loved Scarlet; she loved her a lot, and hoped she would never feel this torture.
"All I'm saying is that it I don't regret trying to love and have a relationship, because now that I did it, I know it's not what I want, and I would have always regretted it if I hadn't bothered"
Scarlet sighed and looked down at her dress. It was true; she had worn it for Connor's sake, hoping he would give her a little compliment, or that his eyes would darken as he looked at her body. Was that pathetic? Or should she do what Busty did and take a chance? Would she be able to live with the guilt

knowing he had a wife at home, wondering where he was.
"I don't know if I could do that to a woman. I'd hate to know that I was the reason a woman had a broken heart." She shook her head "I can't do that to someone"
Busty walked back over to Scarlet, and looked down at her.
"Babe, you have to take care of yourself as well, as you damn well know, no one else will do it for you"
And with Busty's words ringing in her eats, she set off to meet Connor.

Connor couldn't breathe. His collar was too tight, his palms were sweaty and eyes were glued to the vision in front of him. Man, what an idiot he was to even suggest meeting her outside of work! Trust him to get over confident in his ability to be the cold, unfeeling PR agent, and set up this meeting to get the ball rolling. Oh, but Mr. Smarty Pants didn't consider that she would dress up for the occasion, or that the intimate, romantic setting of the restaurant would make her appear to be more gorgeous than she already is.
So far, his cold approach had gone ok, but it wasn't cold enough! She still smiled at him, she still laughed, and he needed her to be angry, not looking at him with desire sparkling in her beautiful eyes.
"So, do you have anymore ideas about this party?" she asked
He swallowed, this was his chance. "No, I'm afraid I don't. My assistant probably has some though"
She laughed lightly "Oh, come on, you remember my opinions about assistants doing all the work"
"Yes, well, I'm a busy man"
"Doing what? Rejecting people all day?" she teased

Damn! Why did she have to know him so well, why did she have to tease him and why oh why did she have to looked at him like he was someone worthy of her.
“Well, I had to meet with a few other clients, they’re business is just as appreciated as yours” he said in his best patronising tone. Aha! It’s working, he thought as her eyes narrowed every so slightly.
“Of course” she replied coolly
He continued “And of course I have other…parties to arrange for them also, so I will have to leave some of the decisions with my assistant. I assure you she is a very capable woman”
“I don’t doubt it” she replied again, in that icy tone.
“But then, at the amount I pay her, she ought to be doing her job correctly” inside he winced. Even to him he sounded like an arrogant prick! Nevertheless he was the least bit happy to see how his plan was working.
Scarlet sat back from the table, her eyes politely folded in front of her, and her face was neutral.
“Of course without receptionists I wouldn’t be able to help celebrities like you, who have a past and need to re-launch themselves.” At the mention of her past, Scarlet’s eyes blazed at him, and he wanted to take the comment back as soon as he said it. It was insensitive to lump her into one category, but he had no other option.
“Such a common case is it then? Having a “celebrity” who had a past?” her chilled tone told Connor how far he had gone.
“Well, many people do yes, whether it’s as little as smoking some drugs or getting abandoned to prostituting yourself out” This was his last carless comment he decided. He couldn’t stand to have her look at him with such hatred, lumping him into the

arrogant PR agents stereotype. The fire blazed in her eyes, showing how angry she was, but her actions were steady as she idly patted her fingers on the table. "Well then Mr Belle, I think we have come to an understanding. Let your assistant handle my party, hopefully we shall see less and less of each other. I assume that's what you want, as you said so yourself you're very busy with other clients who have pasts themselves." She smiled, but it was a fake smile for her eyes didn't glitter; they just looked flat and cold. As she got up he noticed the slight shake to her legs and guilt immediately punched him in the gut. He knew this was the right thing but it didn't stop him from feeling like the world's biggest prick.

Scarlet turned away from Connor and hoped her legs would do their job and get her safely out the door. She held onto her tears until she was free of the restaurant and on the streets. It was only then that she let them fall, mentally hitting herself for being such an idiot! Why, oh why did she even begin to trust that man? She told him most of the hurtful details of her past and he threw them back in her face! As if he thought them the "usual" or that it was common for someone to go through as much pain and rejection as she has. God! What an arrogant bastard! How could he just fob her off onto his secretary! Has she imagined all the flirting and sexual tension between them? Why did he suddenly turn so cold on her tonight, when she'd made an effort and was contemplating an affair with him! So many questions and so many answers lost to her now. Scarlet wiped her tears and walked down the street to her limo awaiting her. Thankfully no press were waiting for her when she got there, she didn't want to have any photographs to remind her of tonight.

Well it was decided now, she wouldn't see Connor again, if she did it would be in passing, she'd deal with his assistant. If that's what he wanted, she'd give it to him. She couldn't shake off the sadness though, that whilst there had been desire between them, they had also had an easy friendship and she would miss the teasing and easy conversation they seemed to have had. No, she reminded herself, that wasn't the real Connor. She must remember that the real Connor is a man who belittles her past and is the perfect stereotype of every PR agent she had encountered. Why did she want to believe that everything he had said was a lie? That it was some sort of game he was playing with her. As Scarlet sat in the limo, looking at the flashing lights whizz by in a blur, she sighed. She might as well accept that she was destined to be on her own in this life. Every single person she had come into contact with had hurt her in some way, apart from Busty and Eddie. She wished Eddie were still here, he would've told her how to deal with a man like Connor. She wondered what it would be like if she had stayed with Peter and been his whore. It would have been degrading yes, but she would've known where she stood. Sex for money. A simple and fair deal. Of course Scarlet knew she couldn't have ever became Peter's whore, the idea of his fifthly, clammy hands on her body repulsed her. Especially after that one night when he had caught her back stage after the play had finished…..suddenly she laughed. If Connor knew the full story the problem of the desire between them would vanish, for he could never want her or love her after he knew the truth. It was a shame she had lived with all her life and it still haunted her to this day. Whenever she felt the familiar sickness swell in her stomach, and her skin grew too tight for comfort, she took a deep breath and hoped it would go away. The doctor said it was panic attacks, hah! It felt more like her body trying to escape itself because it was too ashamed to carry on with this façade she had to live with. She was a celebrity; she had to be perfect no matter what she has to live with, no matter how many secrets lingered in her past. She needed to give the public the perfect appearance, be someone they could idolise and look up to. Why oh why did she ever become a star when she couldn't stand it? Scarlet had never had aspirations to be famous or rich. Her goals and dreams had been modest, along the lines of a warm, cosy family house with a husband and children. Even while Peter had his hands on her, she still believed she could achieve that dream, but now, on the way home from seeing the real Connor Belle; she felt all her dreams plummet to the ground and shatter.

Caroline looked over her appearance before knocking on Connor's study door. She rarely came here, preferring to keep away from him. She wondered what possessed her to seek him out now when they hadn't spoken a word to one another for months now and knew it was John's influence. If she didn't love him....Caroline frowned and shook her head. No, if she didn't love having sex with him she wouldn't be doing this.

The door opened sharply and Connor stood there, his shirt half undone, a tumbler of whiskey in his hand. Honestly he seemed to love that drink which was odd as she thought he would have gone off it since that night...

"Connor" she said coolly.
"Caroline" he sounded surprised, as his mouth hung open a little as he studied her through wide eyes.
"May I come in?" she enquired
That seemed to snap him out of his shock as he straightened, cleared his throat and moved hastily aside to allow her room to enter. "Of course" he said as he closed the door behind her.
"I'm here on a matter of business"
"Um, ok then" he mumbled, putting his glass down and buttoning his shirt. She watched his fingers perform the deft movements and remembered how they had looked on her body. Dark, strong hands on her pale, milky skin. It truly was a shame they had gotten married, otherwise Caroline might have considered keeping Connor as a lover. But once she had became pregnant and he insisted on marriage, it had ruined any pleasure they found with each other. A shame she thought, comparing him to his brother and deciding they were both rather good when it came to the bedroom. Of course, she would never tell Connor this, it was best to remain unfeeling and cold towards him. That way it wasn't complicated.
"Actually it is two matters. First, I have received an invitation from a woman called Scarlet Windsor inviting us and your brother to her...party. I assume she is a client of yours?"
Connor sighed and nodded his head "Yes she is. I haven't seen her for a few weeks though; I know the party is coming up"
"Well I am going to reply and say we are attending."
Connor gulped "You're coming?"

"Of course we need to keep up our appearance of being happily married and in love. No matter how far from the truth that is"
"Well, Caroline that isn't my fault and you know it"
"We don't need to go over this again. What is done is done."
Connor laughed humourlessly "Of course, we don't need to talk about it, we don't need to tell anyone, we don't need this and we don't need that…God sometimes I wonder if you even care what happened"
Caroline looked at him and decided he was half drunk. His words slurred ever so slightly and if he wasn't drunk he wouldn't have dared speak about that night. They hadn't spoken or even mentioned it since it had happened.
"I don't care Connor, but what I do care about is you and me carrying on this lie and doing it convincingly"
He gave a bark of laughter "I'm sure everyone knows how in love we are, I do nothing but talk about how my wife" he spat the word "is the most wonderful woman on God's earth. And how we have satisfying sex every night and how she services me with her mouth" his eyes glittered dangerously as they settled on her face "But of course they would believe me because if I will them to believe they will. That's my talent after all isn't it?"
"What is?"
He clenched his hand tightly "I pretend and act my part so well, no one will doubt me. No one knows who I really am; they just see me as I want them to."
"Which is why our agreement works out so well Connor. Enough of this self-pity, I have another matter and that also includes Scarlet Windsor"

His eyes narrowed again at the mention of her name "What of her?"
"I know you want to be intimate with her and I'm here to tell you that you have to stop it. If people see you chasing some other woman they will know we are not happy"
"We were never happy" he mumbled. Caroline carried on as if she hadn't heard.
"So at this party I need you to be extra attentive and more charming than ever, so this Scarlet woman will get the hint that you are happy"
"But I'm not, Caroline" he said quietly.
"Connor, this isn't about you. We agreed what we had to do six years ago and I've held my end of the bargain up, so do you"
"But you forget, my darling wife," he said as he got up and waked towards her "That six years ago I didn't know the real you, seems you were pretty good at letting people see you as you wanted them to as well." He stopped a few inches from her "You also neglect to remember that six years ago I loved you within an inch of my soul and I would have done anything for you"
She lifted her chin to stare him at him directly in the eyes. "You can't change the past Connor, live with it"
His mouth thinned as he lifted a hand to gently touch her hair. "I loved you so much that I agreed to lie for you to protect you. I could go to the police now, what's to stop me?"
"The fact that your career would be done for"
"I don't care about that anymore, you know that"
She smiled coldly at him. "They only have your word about what happened Connor, I could tell them that it was you that pushed me down the stairs instead of the burglar and that you were the cause for the loss of the

baby. You were so sad about that brat dying; even then people began to wonder if you were involved more than we said you were"
His breath hitched in his throat as rage surged through his veins. "You know how devastated I was about our child. You would use my own grief against me?"
Caroline raised an eyebrow at her husband, daring him to defy her, knowing her threat would keep him in check.
"If that is what it takes. If you want sex that bad, go to a whore"
"Why would I go when I have my whore of a wife right here?"
"I may have been a whore but I would never be one for you again"
Connor suddenly pushed her away, his hands raking through his hair. He spied the tumbler of whiskey and took a gulp. "You never did want our child did you?" he demanded, a hard edge to his tone.
"Why do you want to go over everything now? We've been fine since then"
"No!" he shouted "I have not been fine! I have been dying inside, slowly, painfully and I feel trapped, and the only person who I can talk to, is the person who is killing me!"
Caroline swallowed, chewing on her lips. She didn't feel guilt about Connor; it was just the way it was, why couldn't he accept that and carry on living this façade?
"No, I never wanted our child Connor, I was glad when I miscarried. The brat would have ruined everything"
"You mean your whoring?" his hand tightened on the glass.

“Yes. It would have ruined my life and yours although you think you’re too moral to admit that the child dying was a blessing in disguise”
With a sudden roar, Connor threw the tumbler against the wall, smashing into millions of pieces. He shouted again as he went and lifted his chair, swinging it in mid-air and throwing it into the window. The shattering sound pierced through the house, leaving a still silence in its wake. Connor breathed heavily, knowing he had just reached his breaking point. He regretted lashing out at material things, but he knew himself well enough to realise if he hadn’t he would have hit Caroline instead.
“Get out” he said quietly through gritted teeth.
“I thought you had come to terms with what your life is going to be like.”
“I can’t accept that this bleakness is my life”
“Some people have less than that”
He snorted “You’re thinking of others now Caroline?” he asked sarcastically
“You’re life isn’t as bad as you think. It is what you make it”
He turned to face her “You forget I didn’t make my life like this.” He pointed at her, his finger shaking with unsurpassed anger “You did”
Caroline looked at his finger to him, keeping her face neutral, even though she had begun to suspect this was the beginning of something destructive.

Chapter Five.

John wasn't used to feeling scared. The fear had been beaten out of him by his father, just had the need to cry. His father had made sure that need was brutally trampled down by his belt. John learnt now that he was paying for leaving those emotions dead. For he wasn't the type of man to understand how someone can love another, or how sex could be recognised as a way of expressing emotions. To him, sex was sex. Satisfying for both partners involved, a way of releasing stress. What else could it be?

Which is why John was having trouble coming to terms with this new emotion he was feeling. It unsettled him to no end, and made him feel fear for the first time since he was a child. If John hadn't been the type of man to keep the softer emotions trampled down, he would easily have realised that he was beginning to fall in love and that he cared deeply for Caroline. However, he was not that type of man which is what lead him to turn up at Scarlet Windsor's house one night, with a mind full of fear and a mouth full of false information.

She answered the door to him suspiciously, after hearing from her guard it was Connor's brother, she couldn't fathom what would bring him to her door. But she allowed him to pass the gates and to the house more to settle her curiosity. She hoped she wouldn't pay for it now.

"Yes?" she asked him, taking in his dishevelled appearance. From her understanding John Belle was somewhat an entrepreneur, and he would be seen at various functions or supporting various talents. She had never really made the connection that he was Connor's

brother, but she then she had tried not to think of Connor Belle these past few weeks.
“Miss Windsor, thank you for seeing me, I do realise it is quite late”
“Well, I must admit I am curious as to why you have called on me. I don’t think we have been introduced”
“No, we haven’t, but I am sure you know my brother Connor Belle” the way he stared into her eyes suggested he knew of everything that had happened between her and Connor. Not that anything has happened, she reminded herself.
“Well then come in Mr Belle” she stepped aside.
“Call me John.” He said as he swept past her and found himself in a luxurious, open planned lounge. “This is a wonderful room” he said distractedly as he took in the unusual paintings that hung on each wall, all black and white and gray shades; it had a chilling affect. One picture in particular caught his attention. It was an alleyway between two rows of houses; the houses seemed to cave in on the bright white path, which stood a lone black figure. In the distance you could see the continuing rows of houses as they faded into the white, and as the white moon shone bright in the black sky, it casts many black shadows across the picture, giving it a lonely lost atmosphere. John stared at the picture then regarded Scarlet with admiration.
“You seem surprised” she commented
“I am. I’m afraid I had you labelled as one of those celebrities that either have cream furnishings everywhere or some wild exotic art which frankly looks like a baby got away with his crayons.”
She laughed and he thought it sounded lovely. He could see why Connor had been enticed by this woman, she seemed warm and genuine.

"Well, I do see what you mean. My friend Busty Blackburn has a room full of that exotic art you mentioned"

"Oh" for once John lost his words, not sure if he had insulted her or not.

"Don't worry, I won't tell her"

He smiled, and sat down on the sofa, Scarlet took a chair across from him.

"Ok, you're wondering why I am here. I have to say it is about Connor" at the mention of his brother's name, Scarlet's easy smile fell from her lips. Interesting, he thought something had obviously happened between those two that Connor hadn't told him.

"Oh?"

"Yes. You see, I know about the…possibility of a relationship that is between you"

Scarlet shook her head "No, John I'm afraid you have been misinformed. There is no possibility of a relationship between me and Connor."

"He led me to believe he was besotted with you"

"Besotted?" she asked, her eyes widening. Damn, he didn't want her to feel hope, but the way her face lit up at the fact that Connor had said something about her; well it broke his hard exterior into bits. But no, he was here to protect himself and his easy relationship with Caroline. He needed to remind himself that this woman could be the ruin to everything.

"Well, he said that a few months ago. But he hasn't said anything since then" as her face fell, John felt a stab of something in his chest. Could this be guilt? He wondered. The truth was Connor hadn't stopped going on about Scarlet Windsor since he had met her.

"The thing is, he and his wife are very happy, and I am here on her behalf. They have been going through a

rough patch, and I fear that you coming into Connor's life at this point has confused him. It makes him think he doesn't love Caroline, but he does."
Scarlet felt sick. She didn't need this man coming into her home and telling her about the love between Connor and his wife. Why does he have to rub her face in it?
"I see"
"However, I am a man and I do understand there has been a flicker of desire between you two" at Scarlet's gasp of shock, John headed on "So I suggest that you and him go away for a holiday, get what you have to out of your system, fuck each other within an inch of your lives for all I care, but do it. Then you guys can go back to your own lives"
John smiled hopefully at her, thinking this would be the perfect solution to everyone's problems. Connor would get something out of his desire for Scarlet, he did want his brother to come away with something, Scarlet would have a satisfying week with Connor, Caroline would never know, and he could continue his relationship with Caroline. He didn't even contemplate that Connor could be falling in love with Scarlet and her with him. That was just silly nonsense.
Scarlet looked at John to see if he was kidding. When it was apparent he wasn't when he flashed her that ridiculous hopeful smile, she saw red.
"You want me to be his whore for a week?" never would she be made to feel that way again, not after Peter. For John to even suggest it was insulting even without him knowing her past.
John frowned and as he was about to reply, Scarlet cut him off again.

"No, Mr Belle that is what you are suggesting is it not? Well for your information I will never go and be with someone like that for a week. It is not in my character, but whether it is or not isn't the issue. It is so rude and disgusting for a man like you to come into my room and actually proposition me, but here's the joke, not for himself, but for his brother!"

"Uh…I-"

"No" Scarlet interrupted. She stood up and walked to the front door "You have said enough. I'm sick of men like you, thinking women would actually accept that suggestion. Yes some might, but I will not. The fact that you presume I would without even knowing me speaks of your opinion of women quite clearly. Now, please leave, I suddenly feel as if I could punch something and unless you don't want it to be your face, I suggest you go now"

John got up clumsily, bewildered as to why he was acting like an awkward school boy being told of by the headmistress. He went to the door but before he went out he turned to Scarlet, bringing his face a few inches from her own.

"I'm… sorry" he stuttered before leaving.

Neither of them saw the subtle flash of a camera from a nearby bush.

"I can't believe it" Connor said quietly, looking from the newspaper to his brother. As he had just said, he couldn't believe the picture that had been splashed across the front cover of the newspaper his assistant had given him. He had immediately called John and asked him if he could come and explain what this was all about.

“Well, I thought it the best thing to do for you Con, I was trying to help” he insisted.
Connor narrowed his eyes as he regarded his brother, somewhat surprised to see John looking less composed than usual. He had always seen his brother as the crisp, confident businessman, but John looked on edge today, he kept fidgeting and it sounded as if genuine remorse had crept into his voice. Something Connor had never heard from his brother.
“Why would you offer someone like Scarlet that? Didn’t you know she isn’t the type of woman to accept that? I’m surprised she didn’t hit you in the face”
“She threatened to do it”
That made Connor smile for the first time since his confrontation with Caroline. At the memory of Caroline his smile dropped. He couldn’t believe he had lost it like he had. He had always tried to remain composed when near Caroline and anyone else for that matter, but that night when Caroline had admitted to being glad that their child had died, he had seen red. He supposed it was bound to happen when he suppressed his emotions like he did, but what else was he to do?
“I only thought it would help you out, you could get rid of your desire and Caroline could be none the wiser”
“John, for a smart business man you are stupid when it comes to relationships.”
John shook his head and then looked Connor in the eye “I honestly thought it was the best option”
Connor sighed and tapped his pen on his desk. “And that’s why you can’t do relationships. Not everything is black and white like that John. Whether you admit it or not, you feel emotions like the rest of us”
“No, no I do not”

"John, you're human, which means you feel human emotions. Love being one of them"
Suddenly John shot up, and slammed his hands on the desk "I am not in love. I don't feel anything Connor, if you knew the things I did and things I still do you wouldn't be so sure I was human"
Slowly Connor put his pen down and stared at John thoughtfully, wondering why his brother seemed to be at breaking point as well as himself.
"John, I know you think it's a weakness to feel but-"
"But what, brother? How can I just change what our father made me believe? He drummed into me that emotions were a weakness, while he beat me with his belt he shouted at me for crying, for showing fear, as he believed that was a weakness as well"
Shock appeared on Connor's face "John I-"
"But you didn't know about that did you? He never did that to you, you were his golden boy"
"John, listen to me! No I never knew and I'm so sorry, if I had I would have done something"
"Like what?"
Connor looked blank for a moment "I would have…told mother, or the police, or I don't know"
John sat back in his chair and breathed heavily "Look, I don't know what's happening to me. I'm not usually this…."
"Messed up?"
John looked at his brother and smiled shakily "Yeah"
"Who is the woman?"
John's eyes narrowed his eyes "Woman?"
"Yes, the woman who has you tied up in knots like this. You know Scarlet is my reason, so it's only fair I know yours" Connor smiled teasingly and tapped his fingers on his desk.

"You don't know her. Look I best get off Con, as long as we have this sorted out" he got up to leave and Connor rose as well.
"John, if you need to talk or any help with what happened to you, please come to me"
John looked at Connor for a long time, his gaze hard and mouth set in a grim line.
"I told you, when you find out the things I've done, you'll regret that offer" and with that statement, John strode from Connor's office.

Scarlet picked up her telephone and regretted doing so as soon as she heard the voice on the other end of the line. Connor. Damn why did he have to call her now? She was trying to scrub him from her mind and was doing ok at it. But now he had rung her and all her old feelings came roaring back to life.
"Hey Scarlet"
"Oh, hello Mr Belle" resorting to using his surname would surely give him the hint that she wasn't interested in him anymore.
She heard him sigh. "Scarlet…." His voice trailed off and there was a few moment silence. She was sure why he had rang but his voice sounded like the old Connor she knew.
"Can I help you?" she asked politely, determined to remain aloof.
"Jesus Scarlet, do you have to be so business like?" she had the impression of him running his hands through his hair in frustration.
"I thought that was what you wanted Mr Belle. That is why I have been conferring with your assistant instead of you. It's the *business* thing to do" she put emphasis

on the word *business enjoying* her chance to throw his own words back in his face.
Again there was a few moments silence. "I've missed you" he said quietly. Scarlet stared at the phone, completely shocked at his declaration. They had always been aware of the attraction and growing friendship between them, but neither one had ever voiced anything about it. Connor had taken that first step and it amazed her how relieved she felt that whatever was going on between them had been acknowledge. *Thank god he feels the same way!*
"Did you hear me?"
"Yes" she answered, her voice softening from the cool business woman she had been moments before.
"Well, what…do you think of that?"
"What do you expect me to say Connor? You're married" It hurt to say it out loud, but Scarlet knew she must. She must keep reminding herself that even though they felt something for one another, nothing could ever happen.
"Things….aren't what they seem"
She snorted "Well, you're either married or you're not, Connor"
For the second time in their conversation, she heard Connor sigh.
"It's complicated Scarlet, I mean really complicated. All I know is that I miss you and something is happening between us….I don't know what exactly…"
"Whatever is going on is irrelevant. Nothing can happen Connor, not unless you're planning on leaving your wife"
"I can't do that" he replied bluntly, his tone emotionless.

Scarlet rubbed her eyes, suddenly weary. There was no point to this, she told herself, you're not that type of woman and he certainly isn't the type of man to cheat. "Well then Connor we really have nothing else to say, do we?"

"Argh! Why do you have to be so…so…so-"

"Smart?"

"-Black and white?"

Scarlet thought of all the times in her past where she hadn't been "black and white" as Connor put it. She had learnt the hard way that having hope and allowing emotions to rule was a dangerous game. Thinking back to Peter and how she had believed every promise he had made….thinking he was her saviour…she shuddered at the memory, still imprinted in her mind.

"Connor, having hope that we can or that we could be together would be pointless. I'm sorry; I can't let myself believe all the lies again."

"What lies? I am telling you the truth. Me and Caroline, well…it's hard to explain without telling you…everything…" she heard a bang on the phone "Look, I've been sworn to secrecy, I can't tell you what happened…between me and Caroline, but trust me when I say that we haven't been a proper married couple for six years at the least"

"You could have fooled me Connor. Everyone who knows you always comments on how in love you two are"

"It's all an appearance" he explained, desperately wishing she could understand.

"Of course, the man who makes creating the perfect appearance as a business, is the man who suffers from his own creation"

"Yes! Thank God you finally u-"

"You expect me to believe that? I've heard many excuses from married men before, but this one is definitely unique."
"What do you mean?"
"I would have expected you to say "My wife doesn't understand me" or "We've grown apart" but seriously Connor, I give you points for originality"
"Forget it" he snapped, having enough of her sarcasm. "I thought as a person with a past you would understand that not everything is as it seems. There's a bigger picture Scarlet but you can't or you won't see it because you are afraid of getting hurt. Fine. I'll leave you to your cynicism. I hope its good company" and with that he slammed the phone down. Why couldn't she understand!? The one person he wanted desperately, more than anything and she refused to believe he was sincere. Maybe he did sound like a middle-aged man desperate for a fuck, but she should know him better by now! Shouldn't she?
Connor contemplated this as he squeezed the stress ball his assistant had given him earlier. Even she had sensed he was more tense than usual.
Maybe he demanded too much of Scarlet. It was obvious she hadn't told him everything about her past. When she'd said she wasn't going to believe his lies, he suspected she had mistakenly placed her trust in someone. She probably had ended up hurt, which explains her reluctance to take his word now. But still, he wanted her to understand him; he wanted her to know him inside and out. He…oh God how he wanted her. She represented everything he wanted in a woman, hell even in life. Someone to love and cherish, someone to spend his life with, God knows it wasn't Caroline, that it had never been Caroline. The thought of his wife

caused him to squeeze the ball too hard, his nails digging into his palm. Ever since he had broken down in front of her, she had carried on as if it hadn't happened. Of course, this was Caroline's specialty. He wasn't too surprised to see it occur once again.
Now Connor didn't know what to do. He was going to Scarlet's party, the woman he wanted, with his wife, the woman he hated. And he did hate her. Connor didn't use the word hate; he didn't like to throw it around casually. But the only way to describe his feelings for Caroline was with the word hate. He realised it was dangerous to hate her, because whatever he did to her, he would feel no guilt.

John stared at Caroline writhing on the bed as she brought herself to climax. Yes, he was turned on to the point where his trousers were about to burst, but he made himself watch her. Was this the woman he loved? Truly loved? He had never felt this before and wasn't sure. Did he find her attractive? Yes. Did he get along with her? Yes and no. John had always dealt with Caroline in a clinical way, which is why they used the name Mr. Black. That wasn't love was it? Not even liking to hear her say his name?
She opened her arms, asking him to join her. He stared at her for another moment longer, and then unzipped his trousers, letting them fall and freeing his pulsing erection. Caroline gasped as she looked at him, then a small seductive smile lit her face as she touched her own breast. Did he like the way she did that? Looked at him as if she couldn't wait? Yes he did, he thought as he joined her on the bed, he liked it very much. What red-blooded man wouldn't?

"You feel so good" she murmured as he bent his head and flicked his tongue out to her nipple.
"Are you ready for me?" he asked, touching his own erection. She watched his hand move up and down and licked her lips.
"You know I'm always ready for you Mr. Black"
Inwardly he winced when she used their play name. It reminded him of how cold this arrangement was. Suddenly Connor popped into his head and he felt a slice of guilt cut through his chest. Jeeze, he really was starting to turn human if he was feeling guilt about this arrangement, which had been going on for over a year now.
He felt his lust starting to fade and his erection started to soften in his own hand. He looked down, annoyed more than embarrassed. Caroline must have seen what was going on as she began to crawl down his body, breathing heavily on his, now deflated, penis.
She took him in her mouth, sucking and licking fully. He put his arms behind his head, willing to give Caroline a chance to re-erect him. Connor was a factor he had never liked to think about. He supposed it was because he knew Connor didn't love his wife, so he guessed he wouldn't be too upset about John banging her. But deep down he knew that wasn't true. Connor was one of those rare types of man who didn't believe in adultery and who prized himself on his morals. He wondered if Connor would send those morals flying if Scarlet started sucking his dick like Caroline was doing to him now. At the thought of Scarlet, John felt himself start to respond. Caroline looked up, a satisfied smile on her face.
"I know how to make you arise to the occasion" she said as she straddled him, sliding him into her. John

closed his eyes at the exquisite feeling of him being squeezed tightly. An image of Scarlet rose in his mind as he thrust deeply into Caroline. He imagined it was Scarlet who was sitting on top of him, who was moaning loudly and whose red hair was loose around her shoulders. Suddenly he pictured him and Scarlet in another position. Her on her knees and him pounding into her from behind. Oh…..it felt so good to be inside of her. She would turn her head around and shut her eyes in pleasure as he went deep, making her get even wetter. A moan escaped his throat as he imagined Scarlet shouting out his name as she came, just as Caroline did now, squeezing him even tighter until he climaxed with a shout. John opened his eyes, expecting to see red hair on his bed, but felt disappointment when he saw Caroline's brown hair.

Bloody hell, he thought as he eased away from Caroline and sat on the edge of the bed, I want to be with Scarlet. He looked at Caroline, still recovering from their encounter and cursed himself. He had to fuck Caroline and betray his brother, but now he felt the need to fuck Scarlet sand ruin any chance of happiness Connor could have. What the hell was wrong with him?

Chapter Six

It was the night of Scarlet's big party and she couldn't have felt worse. Everyone was coming and everything had been organised perfectly. But the one thing that wasn't perfect was the fact that Connor was bringing Caroline and she would be forced to see them making lovey dovey eyes at each other all night. Not to mention how awful she has felt since her fight with Connor two days ago. They hadn't spoken since, and she knew it had to be her move if she wanted them to. Maybe Connor had been sincere? Maybe she should have listened to him, at least she should have heard his whole story, and then she could make a judgment. Yes, that's what she as going to do. Tonight, sometime when Caroline isn't by Connor's side, Scarlet was going to pull him aside and ask him. She might just give him a quick kiss…to see if his kissing skills were worth the effort…..No! no she wouldn't do that because that wasn't the honest thing to do.
"Screw the honest thing" Busty had said this evening while they were getting ready together. "Kiss him, have sex with him, do anything with him because I know you girl, if you don't see this through, you'll never forgive yourself" Of course she wasn't going to have sex with Connor, but maybe a quick kiss wouldn't be so bad.
She would have to wait and see what the evening brought.

There was complete silence in the car that drove Connor and Caroline. He wasn't looking forward to this. Not one bit. Caroline was acting her usual, cool, infuriating self and he didn't have the patience tonight.

Connor knew something had to be done with his marriage but divorce wasn't an option. Not unless he wanted every secret he and Caroline have concealed to be ripped out and into the open.

They arrived at the hotel hosting Scarlet's party and walked along the line of photographers, flashing them his fake smile. Caroline did the same, her hand delicately placed around Connor's arm. She smiled, laughed and acted her part perfectly. It made Connor sick.

As they entered the grand hall, he quickly scanned the crowd for Scarlet and was disappointed he didn't see her. A waiter offered him and Caroline a glass of champagne and he took it absently. Then he saw her. She was a sight to behold as her vibrant red hair caught the light and looked as if it went up in flames. She wore a blue dress that hugged her figure and had a delicate diamond necklace that hung down low, stopping just before her breasts. She looked spectacular. So spectacular that Connor found his mouth suddenly dry and his palms sweaty. Great, he probably looked like an awkward teenager standing there gawking at her. He was just about to turn away when she looked directly at him, their eyes meeting and locking. Electricity sparked between them and the air was charged with the sexual tension that always seemed present when they were near one another. He saw her swallow and then bite her lip. He could have groaned at how sexy she looked like that. Her hair wild and loose, her face slightly flushed and her body begging to be loved.

But you're not the man who is going to do that a voice reminded him in his head. No, he wasn't going to sleep with Scarlet, but maybe one kiss….

One quick kiss couldn't be too bad.

"I've been looking for you" Caroline said as she touched John's arm.
He looked down at her hand and decided he didn't like it. He had decided since his imaginings about Scarlet that love was not the emotion he was feeling for Caroline. Lust, definitely. Friendship, maybe and affection, yes. But the big "L" was one thing he didn't feel for her. He wondered why he had gotten so worked up about it, but decided to ignore it. It was easier to ignore the softer feelings than deal with them. That's what strong men did, after all.
"What do you need, Caroline?"
"I need Mr. Black" she whispered.
He looked around; making sure no one was watching them before he answered. "Mr. Black isn't around at the moment"
Caroline's eyes narrowed slightly wondering what had changed John. He had always been up for their games but for the past month or so she had sensed him slowly drifting away. She squared her shoulders, fine, she thought, he can go to some other whore if he wants, but he'll always return to me.
"John, let me know when Mr. Black decides to make an appearance. I'll be waiting" she added as she walked elegantly away.
John watched her walk away, every bit the lady she wanted people to believe she was. What would she do if the tabloids found out the things she got up to? That she was paid for sex and delighted in doing so. He lifted an eyebrow as a plan formed in his mind. He wanted to help Connor get away from Caroline; it would ease his conscious. Did he want his brother to be with Scarlet though? He looked to where she stood,

conversing with a fellow actor and saw how her eyes continually strayed to where Connor stood talking with his assistant. It was obvious they wanted and, God Bless them, needed to be together. For once in his life he could do the right thing….did he want to though?

James Owen and Ben Anthony rocked the place. Everyone enjoyed their music. Comments were made about it being “original” and a “mixture of The Beatles and Neil Young” in a nutshell, the duo were a massive hit. Connor made his way to congratulate them but was sidetracked by a wannabe actress trying to get him to represent her.

“Run along girlie, he ain’t interested” said a voice from behind him. He turned not sure to expect but smiled politely anyway.

“Hi, thanks for that”

“Bet you get that a lot, huh?” she asked, blatantly looking him up and down and stopping when she met his eyes. “Pretty nice”

He frowned “”Pretty nice?”

“Sure. You’re not bad looking for an older man”

“Old?” he repeated, dumbly.

She clucked her tongue “Hmmm, not too smart are you? Scarlet said you were smart”

“Scarlet?” he asked, his pulse racing at the mention of her name.

“Yes. Scarlet.” She titled her head as she looked at him “Do you have a condition that makes you repeat everything?”

He laughed, deciding he liked this refreshing woman. “No. I’m just a bit slow on the uptake.”

“Gotcha. Well, guess I better introduce myself to you and be polite. I’m getting the warning look from

Scarlet" before Connor had a chance to look around for Scarlet; the woman outstretched her hand "I'm Busty Blackburn, Scarlet's best and only friend"
He took her hand, smiling "Her only friend?"
"Well, the only one worth mentioning" she said with a wink.
"Nice to meet you Busty. Scarlet has actually mentioned you one or two times."
Busty put her hand on her hip, her expression one of mock outrage.
"How dare she? Only one or two times? I'm freaking insulted"
"Well, it may have been a few more"
"Hmm, that's more like it. I gotta say this Mr. Belle before Scarlet comes over here and ruins my fun" the teasing glint faded from Busty's eyes and her expression turned serious "Scarlet is like a sister to me. I know all her secrets, as I'm sure you do. She's been hurt badly in the past and I didn't like it. Not one bit. So unless you're serious about her leave her alone"
"I'm surprised she told you-"
"She tells me everything" Busty interrupted.
Connor cleared his throat, determined to be as honest as he could to someone Scarlet cared about. "Busty, I care deeply for Scarlet and I want to be more than friends. The situation with my wife…isn't…the best at the moment, so it is very awkward. But trust me when I say that I don't want to hurt Scarlet. In fact that is the last thing I want to do"
Busty regarded him for a minute or two, and then finally nodded her head as if she believed him.
"I have to say Connor that I was always somewhat curious about your marriage. Caroline's eyes, if you

don't mind me saying, well they're flat. I don't see anything there"

Connor was saved from answering when a familiar voice interrupted him and Busty.

"Bust, what are you going on about now?" Scarlet demanded good-naturedly.

Busty rolled her eyes "I swear she's like my mother rather than a mate"

"Only because you can't look after yourself"

"That's not….." Busty's words trailed off as she looked at the man coming towards her. Lord, he was a handsome man, she thought, he was well muscled (Busty had an eye for these things) but he had the most interesting face. Dangerous, mainly because of the long scar that disfigured the right side of his face, but strangely Busty detected a slight vulnerability in his eyes. No, she must be imaging things.

John's steps faltered when he caught eyes with the petite, gorgeous looking woman who a long mane of blonde hair. She wasn't necessarily skinny, but her body looked well toned and slightly muscled in the red dress she wore. Her blue eyes weren't piercing blue like his brother's but were slightly murky and mysterious.

"Ah, John, nice to see you here" Connor greeted his brother.

John tore his eyes away from the Blonde woman "Hey Con, yeah I wasn't too sure if I would come" he looked back to the blonde "But I'm glad I did now"

Busty snorted "Please that trick is as old as you"

John frowned, taken aback "Trick?"

"You know the one you just did. The way you looked to me before you finished your sentence. Thanks by the way" she saluted him with her glass.

John eyes her thoughtfully, slightly amused. No woman had ever talked to him with such gall, and he discovered he really liked it.

"You're most welcome. I have many other moves and "tricks" as you put them. Maybe I should try them on you as well?"

Busty smiled confidently as she said "Thanks, but like I said they're probably so old I wouldn't even know them"

"Busty" Scarlet said in her warning tone. Busty couldn't help it. Her hands were shaking with the affect this man had on her. She knew who he was of course. John Belle, major player and rich business man. He was also the tabloids recent scoop as they caught pictures of him and Scarlet standing on her doorstep. She knew she shouldn't be so rude to him, but it was her form of defence. No way was he chatting her up then ditching her.

She wouldn't allow that to happen again.

She took a sip of her champagne then saw a casual acquaintance of hers. She thought it was best if she made the escape now, before this man made her more flustered.

"Well, nice speaking with you guys. I'm just going to say hi to those people…over there somewhere" Busty left, glad she didn't look back at John, even thought she could sense his gaze on her.

"Who was that?" John asked as he watched the blonde walk away.

"My friend, Busty Blackburn"

His eyes narrowed "Why have I heard that name before?"

"She was publicly involved with her agent or someone and they dumped her. Very publicly in the tabloids and everything" Connor supplied.
"It was more than that" Scarlet snapped, looking at Connor.
"Sorry Scarlet, I know it was." He turned to John "Busty was desperately in love with this guy and he was a right bastard to her. Used her publicly then chucked her when he met someone better"
"Yes, that's the tabloid version of the story" Scarlet said, tossing her red hair over her shoulder and stalking off.
Connor watched her go.
"I want her so much" he muttered.
John looked at his brother, chewing his lip. Now was his chance to mention his idea. If he played his cards right, maybe he could work this situation to his advantage.
"I have a plan…."

Busty took some time for herself as she ducked behind a pillar and exited through the balcony doors. It had been a long time since any man had affected her the way John Belle had. She knew what he was like though, she did read the tabloids. But even if she didn't his reputation preceded him. He was constantly sexually active; she had heard the gossip concerning him and his bed partners. Sometimes prostitutes, sometimes models, sometimes prostitutes and models. He was a notorious player and Busty didn't want to be another one of his conquests. Even if she did find him incredibly attractive, sexy and mysterious….it was a no go area for her.
Been there, done that.

It was as if they had planned to meet half way across the room when Scarlet and Connor bumped into each other. He was well aware she had been ignoring him all night, ever since his blunder with his words when he had explained about Busty's past to John.
He should have been more sensitive to Scarlet's feelings, but he was always so flustered when she was near.
"If I didn't know any better I'd say you were ignoring me" he said, noting how Scarlet refused to meet his eyes.
"Of course I'm not"
He felt the uncomfortable tension between them and hated it. They had always gotten on so easily and regretted he had acted so cold with her at dinner.
He took a step closer "Look, can we talk?"
She took a step back "We are already"
Connor scratched his chin "Well…can we talk more privately then?"
"About what Connor? We've said all there is to say"
"No, we haven't." he looked into her eyes earnestly, pleading with her to hear him out.
"I just wanted to say how sorry I am for the way I dismissed Busty's ordeal earlier, I know how hard it was for her and I should have had more respect for her because she is your best friend"
She rose her chin "Yes, you should have" then she sighed "but thank you anyway"
He smiled foolishly "Great. Now that's sorted I need to make another apology"
"Oh?"
"Yeah, but I need to do this one…privately"
Scarlet looked around the crowded room. The party was in full swing and it was a massive success. Her

pictures had been taken with every famous celebrity here and hopefully tomorrow she'd be the talk of the tabloids. Ugh, how she hated it.
"I suppose we can go outside if you want"
"Ok, I think that's a great idea" he held out his arm for her to take but she shook her head.
"I'll follow you out in five minutes"
He smiled at her "Worried your dad might catch you?"
That earned him a smile from her which he savoured.
"No, but the photographs of you and me alone on a balcony? Hmm they'll think I'm cheating on your brother!"
"Ok, I see your point, I'll meet you outside. Five minutes, no more otherwise I'll come looking for you"
"Fine, I'll be there"

"I've been looking for you" John said as he stepped from the shadows concealing him and into the light. Busty gave a yelp and turned accusingly on her intruder. Her breath caught in her throat at the sight of John. Damn the man!
"Why's that then?" she kept her voice steady.
"We have something between us"
"You're very presumptuous"
He shrugged "Perhaps"
"You assume I'll fall into your arms?" she asked, her voice dripping with sarcasm
She saw a flash of white teeth in the darkness "Of course, where else would you want to fall?"
"So big headed" she muttered, looking down at her feet.
"Come on Busty, we both know that the tension between us is explosive, and unlike my brother I plan to act on it straight away."

"Maybe your brother is the gentleman" she snapped, ready to defend Scarlet's choice of man.

Again she saw another flash of those white teeth as he stepped closer, too close, invading her personal space.

"Yes, he probably is the gentleman. But we both know that's not what you want"

"You hardly know me"

He shook his head, a frown appearing on his face "I know, yet I feel as if I've known you a long time"

"Another old line" she said, her voice shaking slightly. John must have heard it because he gave her a knowing smile.

"It's true though, something's happening here. And you know it as well. Just listen to your body, feel how it's tingling, feel your heart race at the thought of us having sex"

She swallowed, not allowing him to know how affected her mind and body were by his words. She had to remember this man was a practiced seducer. By next week, she'd be another woman on his long line of them.

"Interesting how you say "having sex" instead of "making love"" she commented.

He lifted a hand and ran his finger down her cheek, "How so?"

She lifted his finger away "Well it sums up what you want quite clearly"

"Would you prefer me to lie and say I love you?"

Her heart soared at the idea. "No" she said quickly, too quickly. "Of course not. I don't know you"

He pulled her to his body, pressing her full length to his. "We could know each other a whole lot better"

Before she had a chance to answer, he swooped his head down and kissed her. Deeply and passionately licking her lips until she opened for him. With a moan of surrender, Busty opened her mouth and let him in. In the back of her head she knew it was the wrong idea, but Lord it felt so good!

This is wrong wrong wrong……

With a cry she jerked away from him, pushing him in the chest so that he stumbled back a few paces.

"No!" she shouted, wiping her mouth as if disgusted.

John straightened up and tried to catch his breath. He didn't like what he was feeling. He was desperately turned on, but also he felt concern that he'd pushed Busty too far and regretted that he might have upset her.

"I'm sorry" he uttered, not used to saying those words. They sounded strange to him but he was surprised to find himself meaning it.

She looked at him and saw genuine regret in his expression. He confused her so much! He should have stomped off by now, pissed that he wasn't getting what he wanted, not standing there looking sorry.

"It's ok"

"No it's not I've…" he stepped towards her again and gently lifted her chin so he could look into her eyes. "I've pushed you too far. I don't know how to deal with someone who…" he stopped talking, mesmerised by her murky blue eyes. They were so unusual and so interesting he could get lost in them.

"You're someone special" was what he finished with. And he meant it; he only had to convince her of that. Hopefully with the plan he and Connor had discussed, he could have Busty as well.

"John…I've been hurt, I don't want to…" she sighed as she gently removed his hand from her chin. She stepped back, knowing it was pointless trying to explain her pain to a man like him. He didn't understand emotions;

he was a man who simply took pleasure from a woman, no strings attached. She wasn't strong enough to have that type of relationship yet.
"Maybe one day I'll get back to you and we can share the type of relationship you want" she said, smiling sadly. Not giving him a chance to answer, she turned on her heel and returned to the party.

Still stunned from his encounter with Busty, John stood on the balcony a moment longer before heading back to the party as well. On the way he saw Connor who explained his plan to meet Scarlet. John wished him luck and left him to it. He hoped his brother and Scarlet had sex tonight that way it would finally prove to Connor his plan could work. He saw Caroline standing across the room talking to a man he didn't know. He saw her put her hand on his arm in that familiar way she did to him earlier and suspected the man was another one of her clients. He wasn't surprised, he wasn't even jealous. He thought back to his last sexual encounter with Caroline, remembering how he had imagined Scarlet. He smiled, acknowledging he was making the right decision in ending it with Caroline. If the woman you were having sex with wasn't enough to make a guy come, then it was definitely time to end it. She wouldn't like it because she'd feel as if she was losing control. Caroline didn't like it when she lost control, which was why after that night six years ago, she had changed. She never lost control anymore; she appeared to be the perfect woman. Cool, calm and collected. She was smart, beautiful and polite. But on the inside, he suspected no one knew the real Caroline. She kept that part of herself hidden. He had to admit this worried him slightly, because if no one knew the real Caroline, who really knew how she was going to react when he and Connor left her?

Caroline was talking to Charlie Edwards, another sleazy PR agent. He was drunk and making a complete idiot of himself. Of course, he thought he was the best thing since Casanova. Which he wasn't. Caroline had shared her bed with many men and she knew this one would be no different from those who had came at her, boasting about the size of their cocks when really they had a tiny one. She had thought it funny the first time it had occurred and had made the mistake of laughing. Her mother had slapped her across the face afterwards "Ya don't ever do that again, you hear me girlie? You's being paid for a service, you gotta do it with a smile." It was another lesson her mother had taught her.
Neither Connor or John knew that her mother had died a few months ago; she didn't care to tell them. She had gotten a call that her mother was dead and she had felt nothing. Not even joy. She didn't think it was strange, John certainly hadn't felt any sadness when his and Connor's father had passed. Well why would he after all the beatings he'd gotten?
Caroline frowned, annoyed that her thoughts kept straying to John Belle. She had many other men she serviced so why did it always come back to him?
"Ya see girlie, I…discovered Mizz Windsor first" Charlie whatshisname slurred, "But she just said "See yah" like some sort of whore."
Caroline's interest sharpened "You two were involved in a relationship?" she enquired slyly, even though she knew Charles wouldn't remember this conversation in the morning.

Charlie Edward smiled "Yeah, she wanted me…bads I say, real bad. I said no no no, I couldn't mix bizz with pleasure, even though the though of her sucking my d-"
"Yes I understand" Caroline interrupted, not wanting the mental image of Charlie and his small penis.
"But, as I says, I says sorry luv, can't help you out. No matter how much she begged for my body, I said no. Gotta remain professional, huh?" he hiccupped and took a swig of his beer.
"Indeed" she replied, thinking it was about time to tell Connor what his mistress got up to.

Katie Micuta

Susie

Susie knew that if Toby found out about this he would kill her for sure. Two years on since that horrible day where he had beaten her until she couldn't see and she still lived in fear. She thought Toby would have gotten better since that night, he might have gotten it out of his system and then they could continue their content marriage. But no. No one would let Susie live in peace. Her life was a game of predator and prey, a game Toby had no intention of losing to. This was apart of her revenge though she admitted it was a shame Toby would never find out.

Lord she was terrified he would find out.

Since that night two years ago, Susie had received a beating on a weekly basis. It seemed to her that Toby had no intention of stopping and he was getting worse. Thankfully he didn't demand that she satisfy him sexually anymore, and if he was ever in the mood he usually pounced on her when she least expected it. The last time had been about two months ago, when she had been cleaning the dishes and he had come up behind her and pushed her forward and lifted her skirt. He had plunged into her crazily for two minutes, then spent himself inside her and walked away. Leaving her standing there naked from the waist down and feeling disgusted. But that wasn't that bad. Susie knew she could survive with him using her for sex, after all men had been using her for that since she was sixteen. But Susie couldn't survive the beatings Toby gave her. Or the fear that the next time would be the last time. Susie couldn't count the amount of times she had woken up in excruciating pain and had wept, wept with joy that she was still alive. Since Toby had started failing to sustain an erection, his rage had become worse. He took it out on her as if she was the reason and blamed it on her for walking in on him masturbating. Susie refrained from retorting that he failed to get an erection because he guzzled whiskey to the point where he passed out. She let him drink as much as he wanted; she enjoyed the few hours' peace she got when he passed out from liquor.

But now, as she laid down on the bed and opened her legs, she wept with fear. For if Toby ever found out she aborted his child he would surely kill her.

Chapter seven

Connor waited anxiously for Scarlet wondering if she would come and meet him. She hadn't appeared too keen, but there was still something between them, he could feel it.
A figure stepped from the shadows and he felt a sense of relief. He started to smile, but it froze on his face when he saw the identity of the person.
Caroline.
The one person he wished it wouldn't be. Why did she always turn up when he started to feel hope.
"What do you want?" he snapped
"Waiting for your lover, dear?"
He snarled at her "Piss off Caroline"
She tutted at him in an infuriating manner "Such vulgar language"
He sighed and willed himself to be patient "So, sorry *darling*, what do you require, *darling*?" he asked sarcastically, spitting out the word "darling" mocking their fake marriage.
She laughed softly "Before you start judging me for my past Connor, perhaps you should find out more about you current love interest"
He stilled "What do you mean?"
"Oh you didn't know?"
"Don't mess with me Caroline, just say what you have to say"
"Your current lover was and perhaps still is involved with her former PR agent, Charlie Edwards"
If Caroline expected Connor to be shocked by this news, she was sadly wrong. He just laughed at her, loudly and unashamedly.

"Oh, Caroline, please. You know better than anyone how people say so many things, but it doesn't make them true." He stepped towards her, towering over her small form. "Scarlet already told me why she left Charlie Edwards firm, because he made a proposition and she refused. You know what type of proposition I mean don't you? You've accepted enough of them in your time."

Caroline remained calm on the outside but inside she was fuming. How dare Connor start making snide comments about her past! It wasn't supposed to be like this, she was the one in control of Connor and their marriage. How dare he do this to her!

"Need I remind you what will happen to both of us if you tell anyone about…night?"

Her husband looked at her with hatred shining in his eyes. She didn't flinch from that look; it didn't matter if he hated her or loved her. Nothing would change.

"I remember Caroline. It's constantly in my head like a chain around my neck"

"No need to be so dramatic"

He gritted his teeth to refrain from retorting, it was best if she just left him alone. Nothing would ruin his moment with Scarlet.

Scarlet approached Connor nervously. She wasn't sure why she had agreed to come and meet him. All she knew was that she would regret it if she didn't see what he had to say.

"Well, I'm here" she said to his back, and as he turned around slowly, a grin spreading across his face, Scarlet was glad she was here with him. He took her breath away and she knew there was something very promising between them.

"I'm glad you came"
"Yes, well, nothing ventured nothing gained and all that stuff" she muttered, wrapping her arms around her waist. His eyes followed the movement and darkened when their eyes met.
"I wanted to apologise" he smiled "I seem to be doing that all the time when you're involved"
"Well that's because you say the wrong things" She could see the intensity in his eyes as he studied her face.
"The thing is I'm confused. I always say the right things; it's what I'm good at. But you…you make me forget my act and allow me to be myself" a small breath escaped him "You have no idea how that feels"
She looked down at her hands, then back up to him "I do Connor, I probably know that just as much as you do"
He took her arm and brought her closer, gently.
"Maybe that's why we get along so well"
"Is that all we do?"
Connor slowly shook his head. "You're so very beautiful"
Her breath caught in her throat "You've never said anything like that before"
He frowned "Maybe I thought I had because I think it all the time"
"You do?"
He laughed softly, stroking her face "You have no idea"
She took hand that was on her face "Connor, I need you to know that if things were different I would be with you"
He put a finger to her lips, stopping her from saying anything else. "Things will be different"

"How do you mean?" she asked, confused.
"I can't say anymore now, but please believe me when I say things will be different, and we will be together"
"But, you love Caroline..." she began and stopped at his bark of laughter.
"No" he said as he shook his head "No I don't."
"But, you always look so happy…"
"Scarlet" he took her in his arms and kissed her forehead. The feel of his lips sent a tingle down her spine. "I haven't been happy for a very long time. Since that night…" his words trailed off as he sighed "My marriage is a sham. It had been for a very long time and I…I was dying inside. But you came along" he smiled as he stroked her hair, looking at the marvellous shade of red, then back to her eyes "You came along with your cynical views on PR agents and your defensive attitude and broke down my appearance"
"Your appearance?"
"Yeah, the one I want everyone to see. It hides the truth"
"Which is?"
"That I am, well I was, a very unhappy man. My life was so bleak I couldn't stand it. I had nothing and no one to speak to. My life was just…empty"
"What about John? Couldn't' you have spoken to him?"
"John…we were never close to be honest, we met out of necessity, brotherly duty and whatnot. But now he's changing. I'm not sure why or what is making him change, but he is changing into a man I can relate to"
Scarlet rested her head on Connor's chest, savouring the warmth of his body and the feel of his arms around her.
"Why were you so unhappy?"

She felt him take a deep breath as he held her tighter. "Caroline is a very…cold and selfish person. She had a hold over me and won't let me go"
Scarlet lifted her head to look into Connor's eyes "What type of hold?"
"I can't say, Scarlet, I want to tell you so much. But the time isn't right now."
"When will you tell me?"
He looked into her eyes as he said "When I know what to do"
"Connor" she whispered "You're asking me to put all my trust and faith in you and you of all people know I'm not good at that"
"I know" he rested his head against hers "But please, you must know how much I want you. How much I need you, Scarlet"
"I don't know" she said unsurely. She saw him frown, and he lifted his head, his thumb stroking her bottom lip.
"Well, let's remedy that" he whispered before he leant forward and gently pressed his lips against hers. It started out as a gentle kiss, both savouring the feeling of each other, both sighing with pleasure. Then Scarlet moaned, and Connor seemed to lose control. He swept her body closer to his, his hand holding the back of her head as he opened her mouth with his tongue, seeking entrance. Scarlet gladly opened up for him, feeling the desire begin to mount to fever pitch. She grabbed his jacket, bunching the material up in her fisted hands, while her tongue battled with his, their kiss now hard, hot and heady.
Connor broke the kiss to bite her neck and then licking away the sting with his tongue, his hand closed around her breast, massaging it while he continued to kiss and

bite her neck. "Connor" she whispered her voice thick with desire and need. Connor groaned at the sound, returning to her lips to take her into another deep kiss. His hand continued to touch her breast, while her own hands grabbed his hair roughly and clawed at his jacket in an attempt to get it off him.

"I need to feel you" he said as he pulled the top half of her dress down, exposing her breasts to his hungry gaze. "Oh god, Scarlet, you are so beautiful"

"Shut up and kiss me" she demanded.

Connor grinned wickedly bending his head to take her nipple into his mouth. His tongue swirled around the tip, his teeth gently nipping around the edges. Scarlet moaned, louder this time, knowing she needed this man as much as he needed her. Suppressed desire sprang forth, causing her to place her hand on Connor's groin. She heard his sharp intake of breath, his other hand finding her other breast, fondling the nipple.

"Connor, you feel so good" she said as she moved her hand back and forth over his erection, squeezing gently, urged on by his moans of delight and pleasure.

Suddenly his head lifted, his breathing ragged and they looked at each other. They saw their own yearning reflected in each others gaze, both knowing this was what they wanted, what they needed.

His hand trailed slowly down her body, from the middle of breasts to her flat belly, then dipped lower, touching her where she craved it the most. Her eyes closed and her head fell back at the feeling of his hands rubbing her.

"I need to feel you on my fingers" Connor said as he lifted her dress with one hand and brought his other up to her thigh to the appendix of her thighs. She gasped at

the feeling of his cold fingers moving over her wet warmth.
His thumb found that little nub of pleasure, and he began to rub it back and forth like she had done to him. She opened her eyes and looked at the stark desire blazing in his eyes, his need as fiercely as hers.
"Touch me" he gasped. Her hand moved down to his trousers and unzipped them enough so her hand could get through. She then felt his throbbing erection, and slid her hand over it, gently at first, but then she increased her pace until he was gasping.
Connor returned to sucking her breast and as he nipped at the nipple, he slid a finger into her wet passage. Scarlet moaned loudly, loving the feeling of his fingers on her.
"Keep going" she urged, the fever pitch burning higher and higher "Faster, Connor, faster" he increased his rhythm, rubbing her clit while sliding his fingers in and out of her. Suddenly her body stiffened, and she cried out, her hand still pumping up and down Connor's hard cock. The sound of Scarlet reaching fulfilment was Connor's undoing. He shouted out, and came all over her hand, holding her tightly as the spasms subsided. Their breathing ragged, they stayed embraced together, enjoying the feeling of being held. Something they both hadn't experienced for a while.

Eventually Connor made himself pull away from Scarlet even though he loathed doing so. He kissed her tenderly, gently on the lips and pulled away. He took out a tissue from his pocket and handed it to her. They didn't say anything as they cleaned themselves and made themselves presentable. When they were both ready Connor smiled at her and held out his hand, she

took it and they walked together to the edge of the balcony doors.
Scarlet turned towards him before they returned to the party. "Connor, before we go back in there where we have to act like nothing happened, I want you to know" she paused and brought his hand to her cheek "That what happened between us is really special and I'll wait for you"
Connor couldn't reply as emotion burned in his chest. All he did was take hold of Scarlet and bring her body close to his for one last, sweet kiss.

As the party died down, the guests began to depart. Everyone thanked Scarlet and professed to have a brilliant time. Scarlet watched as Caroline and Connor left, her hand around his arm. The pain sliced through her, but she knew she had to be strong and trust him. Busty helped Scarlet settle everything with the caterers and waited for her friend to join her.
"We shall meet again" a voice said behind her. She didn't have to turn to know it was John Belle speaking.
"We may. We may not" she said as she turned around, a sweet smile pasted on her lips.
He gave her a mocking smile. "Busty, we both know what will happen"
"Enlighten me"
He stepped forward so he could whisper in her ear "Wait and see" Then John turned around and strode towards the exit. Busty stared after him at a loss for words.
"You like him" Scarlet said from behind her
Busty turned "Nope"
"What crap." She laughed and took Busty's arm "I know you and I know that look you have in your eyes"

"Please, give me some credit, Scar, the man basically told you to have an affair with Connor instead of something more meaningful. That sums him up. He's after sex and that's it."

Scarlet shook her head, her tone turning serious "No Busty, I think he is serious. Thing with John Belle, which is the same as his brother, he wouldn't pursue someone if he didn't truly want them"

Busty snorted "He likes the chase"

"No, men like John don't need to chase. They are the chased"

Busty pondered that for a minute "Ok, then answer me this. So say John and I had sex, and it was fantastic-"

"How do you know?" Scarlet interrupted

Busty winked back "Men like that just have a certain charisma. I just know he'd be awesome between the sheets"

Scarlet laughed at her friend, putting on her coat as they reached the doors. "Ok, carry on with what you were saying"

"Right. So say we had sex and it was great, what then? Good sex for a few months?"

"Could be worse"

"I'm not ready for that. That's not what I want to do"

"Then don't. I'm just saying, I think he could be the type of guy who might be capable of more"

"Come on, remember his reputation?"

"Appearances aren't what they seem" Scarlet said with a small smile, remembering how Connor had confessed that his and Caroline's relationship was a sham.

Busty still looked sceptical "We'll see. I'll go out with him, once. Then I'll let you know"

"Ok," Scarlet said as she linked arms with Busty "Deal. You know I'll hold you to that, right?"

Busty laughed “I’m counting on it”

Chapter eight

Caroline was a woman who loved being in control. She hadn't always been in control of her life; she hadn't ever been given the chance to. Her mother had raised her to be the type of woman she's wanted her to be. She'd taught Caroline the lessons she'd wanted her to learn and had never asked what Caroline had wanted. Caroline supposed it was good the way things had turned out because if she hadn't met Connor she would still be living a life that someone else controlled. One lesson she had learnt in life was that everyone took their freedom for granted. People only noticed it was gone when someone took it away, exactly how Connor had discovered. She hadn't intended to ruin Connor's life and still believed truly believed she hadn't. Connor had a good job and lots of money, everyone considered him a gentleman and....well, Caroline couldn't think about everything he had, but she was sure he had more than that. The only thing she asked of him was to keep her secret and remain married to her. Was that too much to ask? No matter that she didn't have sex with him anymore and wouldn't allow him to see anyone else. No matter that the secret he kept was actually her fault and no matter that while Connor felt heart wrenching loneliness she was having a relationship with his brother.

No matter at all.

Although now Caroline was angry. After six years of keeping her secret and keeping his mouth shut, Connor was now starting to act out like some hormonal teenager. She shuddered to think she could have had a six year old child now if that burglar hadn't pushed her down the stairs. She'd have to tame Connor again,

perhaps with a new threat. She frowned; concerned that he hadn't heeded her last threat about telling everyone it was he who pushed her down the stairs instead. He simply didn't seem to care anymore.
And she knew that was the most dangerous problem of all.

"So, do you think this plan will work?" Connor asked as he signalled to the waiter for another whiskey. John eyed his empty glass thoughtfully.
"You do know if you keep drinking like that, you'll get a liver problem"
Connor snorted "Sure, thanks Dr. Belle"
John shrugged "Hey, I'm only saying"
"Why do you care?"
John looked at his brother, unsure of how to answer that. Why did he care? He'd never been one to care about his brother, usually they met out of some sort of family duty, but now he actually meant what he said. He found himself wishing Connor was happy with Scarlet and that he was happy with Busty. And didn't that girl stir some new emotions up! She was gorgeous, witty, sharp, did he mention gorgeous? John felt himself suppressing the urge to pick her up and hug her tightly to keep her safe. Then she made him want to start undressing her, touching her until she felt good….John had always seen to his bed partners satisfaction but had never wanted to make them feel good. With Busty he wanted to make sure she knew how gorgeous and sexy she was and how much of an idiot that man was when he let her go. Damn her! He felt so different now after meeting her and knew she was one of the reasons he was feeling….emotions.

"Of course I care, Con, you're my brother" he answered, for the first time truthfully.
Connor stared at him in shock but then broke out in a grin. "Jeeze, John. You know, I liked Busty before but since you've met her, you've changed a great deal"
"I know and it feels really good" he answered sincerely.
"What do you think will happen?"
"Happen?"
"Yeah, you're going out with her tomorrow night, aren't you?"
John nodded "Yes, I'm taking her out"
"Well, are you going to make a move or…something?"
He shook his head "No. I want her to know I want the real thing with her. I usually just have sex with women then leave them, with her it's different." John sighed and looked into empty space "I want to have my first proper relationship with her"
Connor slapped him on the back in a well-done-mate kind of way.
"John, that's brilliant! I'm glad for you. Busty is a really nice girl as well, just be gentle and slow with her." He warned "Scarlet said that Busty is still raw from the whole break up thing"
John nodded. They both remained silent thinking about their own women when John said "How's Scarlet?"
Connor got that faraway look in his eye when he spoke of Scarlet "She's great. We've met a few times, you know in a private place were no cameras are, but man, John I need more"
"More?"
"Yes. I need to be with her. All day, every day"
"Aren't you participating in….heavy petting?"

Connor grinned sheepishly "Yes, yes we are. And jeeze I need and want to go further. But it's not just that though. I want to be in a real relationship"
John nodded, for the first time in his life understanding what his brother was saying. "Well, if the plan works it will happen."
"When shall we…put it into action?"
John stroked his chin as he thought. "We need to make sure Caroline doesn't have anything else over you Connor."
"What do you mean?"
"Well, we both know what happened six years ago. I know all the gritty details just as much as you do. So when you say you're leaving her she'll threaten you, claiming you pushed her or beat her but then I'll step in and I'll let her know that I'd vouch for you if she ever told anyone a lie of what happened"
"Will that be enough?"
"As long as you're sure you don't care about your career endings or being hurt by gossip, then yes, I think it should be enough." John stared at his brother, hoping his words were true. Connor still didn't know about his and Caroline's relationship and knew when she found out that not only was Connor leaving her but he was as well, that she would not be happy. He tried to imagine the worst thing she could do to him and Connor and came up with spreading malicious gossip. Nothing too bad; he could deal with gossip.
John would do well to remember that he shouldn't underestimate Caroline.

"You look lovely" Scarlet said, staring at Busty.
"Are you sure it's not too full on?"

"I don't see why you'd think that. It's what you usually wear"
"Yeah, but what I usually wear is battle gear"
Scarlet laughed and took Busty's arm, leading her to the doorway. "Look, it doesn't have to be like that with John. Connor told me that his brother was talking seriously about you and how much he has changed since he met you"
"Really?"
Scarlet rolled her eyes "Yes"
"Scar, I don't want to get hurt again"
"Nor does John, so why would he hurt you?"
Busty looked at Scarlet. "John was hurt?"
"Damn" Scarlet sighed and shook her head "I didn't want to tell you, but well, John was beaten as a child by his and Connor's father. He was basically taught to suppress emotion and show nothing"
Her eyes narrowed "That's pretty specific. How do you know all this about him?"
"Connor told me. Connor had only just found out after John told him. For some reason John kept it a secret from Connor and everyone all these years."
"The scar…"
Scarlet shrugged "I don't know. I think it must have been something to do with his father. Connor never told me anything about that"
"Well…I guess everyone's been hurt in some shape or form"
"Yeah, Busty, it seems they have"
Busty shivered and smiled at her friend "Jesus, enough of this depressing talk. I'm going to go out to dinner with John, get to know him and who knows?" she asked, her eyes twinkling; a twinkle Scarlet hadn't seen for a long time.

Connor felt excitement running through his veins as he waited for Scarlet to answer the door. When she did, he didn't give her time to talk. He strode in, backed her up against the wall and kissed her soundly. Their kiss instantly turned as needy and as hot as their others did and not before long Scarlet was pushing his jacket off his shoulders and Connor was lifting her so she could wrap her legs around his waist. He rubbed the centre of her against his swelling erection, hearing her gasp and encouraging him to continue. She reached down and undid his trousers, releasing his hard cock and touching it with a firm grip. "Scarlet" he whispered, returning to kiss her mouth.

Somewhere in the haze of desire, Scarlet heard her telephone ringing.

"Ignore it" Connor said, still continuing his seductive assault. The phone continued to ring and ring, and then finally when it stopped and allowed them a ten second moment of silence, it began to ring again. Connor groaned, finally giving up and allowing her legs to slide down his body.

"Sorry" she murmured as she took a deep breath and went over to the phone. "Hello?"

"Hi there, is this Miss Scarlet Windsor?" asked a make voice on the other end.

"Yes it is"

"Great, I was wondering if we could get a statement from you to publish in our monthly magazine *Timescale*"

"Ok yes, I'd be happy to" she glanced at Connor and saw he had buttoned up his trousers and was sitting on her sofa.

“It’s about the time when you were abandoned. I’m wondering if you’re willing to speak about a man called Peter Guild”
Scarlet’s face turned pale as she heard the name of the man she had been trying so hard to forget.

“Hello, Miss Windsor?” the voice asked on the other end of the phone. Connor picked it up from the floor where Scarlet had dropped it.
“Hi there, this is Mr Belle, Miss Windsor’s PR agent”
“Ah wow, it’s a pleasure speaking with you-”
“Yes. Well, she’s just been called away because”
Connor looked over at Scarlet who now sat on the edge of the sofa. “Her friend has called over”
“Oh, ok. So you’re at her house for a social call?” asked the annoying voice.
Connor knew he was getting himself into trouble. He’d bet his last pound that tomorrow there would be an article on how “Mr Belle was visiting Miss Windsor last night around her house. Perhaps they both like to mix business with pleasure!” It sickened him to think that there was no privacy anymore.
“Yes, it is a social call” he put the phone down before the annoying voice asked him anymore questions. He looked at Scarlet knowing they would have to talk about her past again. He knew she would admit to resorting to prostitution to make her way in the world, but now Connor knew it didn’t matter. He’d want to be with her no matter what she had done.
He knelt down beside her and took her hands “Scarlet, honey, talk to me”
She looked at him, a frown creasing her beautiful face “I can’t”

"Tell me about this Peter guy, tell me what you had to do to survive"
She got up and wrapped her arms around herself, her back facing Connor.
"It wasn't like that. I believed he loved me" she said quietly.
"You were in a relationship with him?"
"No. Although he led me to believe we were, or that we could be."
"Tell me" he urged. She felt him stand behind her but he didn't touch her. She was grateful because if she was going to tell him all about Peter, she needed to do it. She didn't want Connor's kindness or gentleness, not when she told him about what Peter had done. She was disgusted with herself and knew Connor would turn away from her when she told him the truth. Was she ready to face his rejection?
She turned to look at him and the tenderness in his gaze nearly broke her down. She wanted to curl up in a ball and have him hold her close, to protect her from her painful past. Realistically she knew she couldn't do that, so instead she stepped away from him. She knew she had hurt him from his wounded expression but smiled at him to reassure him. "Con, I need to just…get it out without any distractions"
He nodded and stepped away to sit on the edge of the sofa, looking up at her expectantly.
"You know that I started working with Peter. He wasn't my boss, he was just a fellow worker you know?" at Connor's nod she continued "But he always let me know he wanted to be…more than a fellow actor. First of all his attempts were really sly and…he was just acted like a smug male, telling everyone I was begging him for a shag. A lot like Charlie did" she smiled and

looked down at her fingernails. "A lot of the people ignored him, knowing what he was like, but most importantly knowing that I wasn't that type of girl." She looked at him "I hadn't been out with anyone; I just preferred people to leave me alone"
"You were a loner" Connor said, a small smile forming on his face.
She smiled at him warming at the smile he gave her. Maybe he could cope with her past; maybe he wouldn't turn his back on her.
"Anyway, people didn't take any notice of his ramblings, and eventually everything died down. Peter left me alone and I carried on acting as an extra. Once I even acted as Beatrice in Much Ado About Nothing. I was so happy! She was my favourite character and it was just the type of acting break I wanted. Everyone was pleased for me and they helped me rehearse lines and helped teach me stage directions. It was then when Peter began to be nice. Gone was the sly smug male he once was and he just seemed to be a really genuine, nice guy. He once asked me out for a drink and I agreed"
Connor's fists clenched with jealousy at the thought of Scarlet going out with another man. He took a deep breath, willing with himself to remain calm; he didn't want to stop Scarlet, not when he could sense she was getting close to the painful part of her memories.
Scarlet carried on talking, unaware of the emotions swirling inside Connor. "We actually had a nice time" she laughed mockingly at herself "He was the perfect gentleman. We laughed, we joked…we jus had a great time. He asked if he could walk me home and I once again said yes." Scarlet shook her head, her hand pushing hair out of her eyes "I was so naïve, I just

though he wanted to make sure I got home ok. He walked me to my door, I said thanks and started to opened it and go in. I felt his hand on my shoulder and turned around expectantly." She looked at Connor, sadly "I thought he wanted to tell me something"
"Scarlet" he whispered, an image of a young, hopeful woman rose in his mind and he felt anger at Peter for ruining her hopeful view of the world.
"He tried to….he touched me, pawed at my breasts, and just trapped me between him and the door. I panicked so much, not knowing what to do. Have you ever felt so much panic and shock that your body just….it just….stops. It was as if I was paralysed, I couldn't move." Connor nodded in agreement, knowing how she had felt. He remembered to six years ago when the shock and surprise had held his body hostage. Scarlet carried on as if Connor hadn't moved. "I eventually came to my senses when I felt his fingers on my….well you know. I brought my knee up into his groin and he doubled over with the pain. I remember that I fumbled with the lock, trying to get in desperately and I nearly did." Scarlet dashed away the tears forming in her eyes "I was just about to shut the door when his…his foot stopped me from closing it. I shouted with fear, some nonsense like "I'll call the police" but he just laughed at me." Scarlet took a shaky breath "I tried to push at the door but his strength was superior to mine. Eventually he got in and pushed the door so hard that I fell over and tumbled to the ground. Before I had a chance to get up, he was on top of me, ripping my clothes, trying to feel my skin." Scarlet started walking back and forth across her lounge; Connor followed her with his eyes, desperate to comfort her. "I shouted "Leave me alone" and he hit my face. The pain, oh God the pain hurt me

so much. I remember that he laughed at me again, the sound so cruel I can still hear it sometimes. He found my bare skin and shoved his finger inside me, plunging in and out, his rough skin and jagged fingernails hurting my insides. I must have started bleeding from it because Peter looked at his hand and gave me a disgusted look. I shouted at him again to get off me, he didn't listen. He fumbled with his trousers and freed his…small dick" Connor smiled reassuringly at her "I felt him hover and then he just…he…forced himself inside me." Scarlet let her tears fall as the memories swarmed her mind. "Connor I was so frighten, I didn't know what to do to get him off me. Even while he was…doing his thing…I tried to bring my knee up but he clamped them down with his arm while the other held my arms above my head. I had no escaped. Eventually when he finished, he just rolled off me and got up. He did his trousers up as he looked at me. I scrambled away from him, trying to hide my nudity, but there wasn't much I could do as he ripped all my clothes. I remember that I looked him in the eyes and told him to get out. I said it quietly but I knew I sounded serious. He must have known it to because he fled my apartment quickly. He didn't return to work the next day and I never saw him again. No one else knew about what had happened; I was too ashamed." Scarlet looked at Connor, letting him see her tears. "It was then when I promised myself that I would never let a man take advantage of me again. You say I turned cynical, well perhaps I did, but it was the only way. I haven't let anyone close to me apart from Busty because people always leave me. They use me and then leave me, and Con, I can't cope with it anymore. This is why I have

trouble trusting you and letting you in, too many people have taken advantage and I don't want to be hurt again"
They both stared at each other, tears running down Scarlet's face and stark tenderness showing in Connor's expression.
Scarlet was terrified Connor was going to turn away from her, but one look at his expression caused her to groan with relief. She closed her eyes and let her tears fall feeling his arms come around her body and holding her tightly. She sobbed violently, knowing Connor was there to support her.

In a restaurant across town there was another meeting taking place. Busty and John didn't share their emotions as much as Connor and Scarlet, but they felt them just to the same intensity. Busty was surprised that she and John got on so well. They joked and laughed and made easy conversation. She saw a new side to John, an easy carefree side which she found herself liking immensely.
"So, what do you think of Con and Scarlet?" he asked as he took a sip of his drink. Busty took a gulp of wine, her eyes dancing with mirth as she looked at him over the rim.
"Oh, you know," she answered casually.
He leant forward "No, tell me."
"Well, it should be all ok. I think Scarlet is into your bro, big time. I just hope that witch doesn't get in the way"
John sat up straighter, guessing who Busty meant but asking anyway "Witch?"
"Caroline." She swallowed "I mean, I get that after losing a baby it changes you, but her eyes are so lifeless"

"How do you mean?"
"Well, she just looks as if she feels nothing. She acts her part quite well, the smiling, happy wife of Mr Belle, but her eyes…they give me the chills."
John looked at Busty, the woman he was starting to suspect he was falling in love with. Everything about her looked like she was the perfect woman. Of course he knew she wasn't the perfect woman but she was probably very close to perfect. The problem John found himself facing now was the fact that if he was falling in love with her, he needed to be honest. He felt this urge to be straight with her and to tell her everything about him. Including his affair with Caroline. John didn't relish that task but he knew it had to be done if he wanted an honest, open relationship. John silently laughed at himself, amazed at the change in him. Six months ago he wouldn't have recognised himself.
"Busty, there are things you need to know." He cleared his throat "If we're to get….involved"
"Whoa! Who says we're getting involved"
John smiled confidently at her. "I do"
She raised an eyebrow at his manner "Oh, and I suppose everyone just does as you want them to then huh?"
"Of course they do. Come on Busty, for a minute stop with the defensive act and sharp wit. Just talk to me" his expression turned serious as he looked into her eyes "I'm interested in you. But as you might have heard, I have a certain past"
"I've heard about your conquests"
For once in his life, John regretted the way he has lead his life, meaningless encounters with woman, treating them as nothing but away to pass time and keep his boredom at bay.

"I do admit I've been with numerous women."
She scoffed "Many women"
He smiled a little "Ok, ok, many women. But I've changed." He held up his hand "I know you've probably heard that excuse a thousand times but it is true. I…I've been a selfish and empty man most of my life, when I was young I was taught not to show emotion; that it was a weakness. My father, well he beat me whenever I showed anything that he considered weak" John smiled wryly "It worked, I never showed emotion. Instead I isolated myself from a relationship with Connor or a relationship with a woman." He took her hand across the table, looking into Busty's eyes. "The reason I was with so many women was because I was frustrated with myself. I had no other…way to express myself. So I did it through sex"
"John," she said softly, squeezing his hand "You don't have to tell me about your past. Because it's exactly that, it's your past."
"But I want you to know me"
"I will. We just have to give it time. We gotta date like normal people"
"Busty, I'm not like normal people though." He sighed "This scar" he gestured to his face "It's hideous but it's a constant reminder of who I am and what I was moulded into."
"How did you get it?"
"My father whipped me with the belt on a daily basis, but one day he was completely drunk and his aim was off." At Busty's gasp of shock he brought her hand up to his lips and kissed it "Don't worry. It didn't get my eye, but it was bloody close I tell you. Whenever I see it though I remember who my father moulded me into

being and I feel sick with myself when I think of the things I've done…done to those I love."
Busty looked at him, confusion obvious in her gaze. She didn't ask for John to tell her about his past, but was so glad he had. It showed her he was serious about her and that he trusted her enough to let her in. She wondered if they were going too fast which was why she had suggested dating instead, but knowing John this intimately felt right to her.
"What have you done, John?"
He looked up at her question and seeing sincerity in her gaze, he was willing to take a leap.

When Scarlet's sobs subsided Connor still help her close, keeping her warm.
"I'm so glad you didn't run when I told you"
He kissed her forehead "You thought I'd run from you?"
"Not many men would still want a woman after they found out she had been raped"
He grabbed her chin firmly yet gently, so she looked into his eyes. "Scarlet, you know me. You know I wouldn't run from you, whatever you did"
She smiled and lifted her hand to cup his cheek "I do know. It was just a horrible part of my life and I didn't want it to ruin what we have"
"Nothing will"
"Not even Caroline?" Scarlet couldn't resist asking. After baring her soul to the man she loved she felt as if he could do the same now.
Connor rested his head on the back of the sofa "Scar, you know my situation"
She lifted her head "You see, the thing is I don't actually know. Yes I know you have a secret between

you and Caroline and you can't leave her because of it, but I don't know what the secret is or why it stops you from leaving her"

Connor sat up, causing Scarlet to sit up as well. He turned towards her, keeping hold of her hand. "I'm working on a way to get out of it. John is going to help me. Then we can be together."

Her heart soared at the thought that they could be together. "You do?"

"Sure. It was John's idea actually. He…well he has this idea and we're going to try it"

"When?"

"Soon" he promised, kissing her hand.

They remained silent for a while, just enjoying each other's company.

"So, you will tell me the secret when you can?"

Connor groaned as he got up and stood staring down at her. "Scarlet, can't you just let it be?"

"Connor, in case you haven't noticed, I'm falling in love with you here. You know my issues with trust and I'm trying my hardest, honestly I am, but the fact that you go home to her every night, even though I know you're not with her, is still a difficult fact to deal with"

Connor heard what Scarlet said, but he couldn't reply because of the wild thumping of his heart. She said she was falling in love with him. He was completely stunned.

"You're falling in love with me?" he repeated

She huffed. "Yes. I am, so you can just remember that the next time you get impatient with me"

A grin broke out over Connor's face, lighting his eyes, making them sparkle with happiness. "Scarlet, I can't believe you're falling in love with me"

"Why wouldn't I?" she asked, her heart warming at the sight of Connor looking so happy.

"I imagined you saying those words but I never expected you to actually say them. Do you know how happy you make me?" he asked as he picked her up and twirled her around. Scarlet smiled, unable to resist Connor when he was this happy. She laughed and giggled and grinned broadly, hugging him to her. Hope flared in her chest as she held the man she loved closely. Maybe everything would turn out exactly as she wanted them to.

She hoped.

Susie

This was the last time. The last time she would allow Toby to beat her. Her plans were set in motion and she would leave him in a few short weeks. Since the abortion Toby had thankfully not come near her with sex in his mind. Their relationship was purely predator and prey, and she was sick of being the weak. It had taken a long year for her to put her plans into motion, but she had finally did it and now the day was looming. Although Toby didn't use her for sex anymore he still expected her to make his food. Which worked as a blessing in disguise. The small boy, Jack had helped her acquire a sleeping remedy. Well the boy Jack told her it was a sleeping remedy but she wasn't too sure as she had never needed to buy sleeping remedies before. If Susie was honest with herself, she didn't care what medication she was giving Toby as long as it made him sleep through her departure.

In the last year Susie had grown into a woman, a woman who had decided it as time to get out of this relationship. She wasn't dumb though, she knew she couldn't just walk out of a relationship and into the big, wide world without any money or anywhere to go. But she had taken care of that. Once Susie had felt disgusted that she had been used for sex by numerous men in her lifetime but then she had realised that she could use it to her advantage. Men were easily led by their cocks; why not use her knowledge to her advantage? Susie had already met another man and had already made him smitten with her. He was awaiting her arrival at the coffee shop where they had met at. When he had approached her she acted withdrawn and

uninterested, but as he preserved and kept trying to coax a response out of her, she felt herself warming to the man. He had a nice laugh and was willing to help her out of this mess. But, he didn't know she was married or trapped in an abusive relationship. She didn't think that was what men wanted to hear. So she hadn't told him but did intend to leave Toby as soon as the drug took effect on him. She planned to slip it into his dinner tonight, then leave and meet her new man and the new life she would have with him. She knew it wasn't a love match; she didn't believe such a thing could exist after being treated as badly as she had. But Susie knew she would be safe.
Anywhere was safe apart from here.

That night Susie left Toby Shore. She had slipped the drugs into his food and he had eaten without any suspicions. She left through the back door, carrying a plastic bag which contained three dresses and two pairs of socks. Those were the only items of clothing Toby had given her in the last four years.
Susie crept away quietly, hoping no noise gave her away. Soon she stepped out into the darkened street; the winter weather had arrived with a vengeance and it was bitterly cold.
She looked back at the rotting cottage which had been her prison for the past four years and suddenly smiled. She knew she was going to be ok now she was away from Toby.
He couldn't hurt her anymore.
How wrong she was.

Chapter nine

"Tell me how it went" Scarlet repeated for the tenth time that night. Busty had been mysteriously quiet about her evening with John and she was beginning to get suspicious.
"No"
"But, we always share the details. That's what makes us friends" Scarlet pouted at her friend.
"No, don't use that pout on me. And don't guilt trip me! This meeting with John was private"
"Did you guys do it?"
Busty rolled her eyes "Please, what a question"
"Well, it's not that unusual Bust, you usually do"
"Thanks!" Busty grabbed a pillow and threw it at Scarlet, who was sitting opposite her in the arm chair. Scarlet laughed and caught the pillow with ease "Ok, ok, don't tell me. But I'll have you know I have some juicy gossip as well"
"You do?"
She nodded "Yup, but I don't know, I can't tell you" Scarlet smiled cheekily and had a sip of water.
Busty smiled but then looked down at her clasped hands. "I can't tell you Scar, it's a secret"
Scarlet's smile dropped. "Fine. So now you're in on the secret between Connor and his wife?"
"No!" Busty sat forward and rubbed her eyes "It's not that secret. It's one about…John's past that's all"
"Oh...so you told you everything?"
Busty nodded "Yeah. He said he wanted me to know the real him and that he's looking for a serious relationship with me"

Scarlet squealed with delight and got up to sit next to her friend “Busty! That’s brilliant!” she looked at Busty’s sombre face “Isn’t it?”
“It is, but Scar, some of the things he’s done…I mean, I know he says he’s changing and that Connor sees a change in him, but….he’s used women in the most awful way, just as…”
“Just as your ex did to you?”
“Yes” she looked at Scarlet “And worse. He’s had affairs with married women…and how do I trust someone who has done that?”
Scarlet smiled gently at Busty and took her hand in hers. “Listen, you can’t know he won’t. But, trust me when I say I think John is changing. The fact that he even told you about his affairs on the first date shows that”
“How so?”
“Well, a man wouldn’t tell that to a woman and risk the possibility of making her run away if all he wanted was to use you would he?”
Busty slowly nodded her head agreeing with Scarlet’s reasoning. “He wouldn’t if all he wanted was sex”
“Exactly. So trust him Busty, just give him a try”
Busty remained silent, thinking back to three nights ago when John told her about his affair with Caroline. He had said it quietly, as if he was ashamed of his actions, but Busty knew that could be an act. He had sworn her to not tell anyone because Connor didn’t know.
“Aren’t you going to tell him?” she’d asked John as he stared down into his empty glass. He’d looked up at her and she was captivated by the vulnerability and fear that was obvious in his eyes.
“I don’t know” he’d answered. “Caroline was just a woman I used. I didn’t chose her to get back at Connor,

I didn't chose her because I wanted to hurt anyone, she was just a woman"
"She's your brother's wife" she'd hissed
"But that didn't mean anything to me!" John had rubbed his eyes and sighed "Being married or being in a relationship didn't matter; it was all the same thing. *Women* were all the same thing."
"Sex" Busty had said quietly, looking up at John. He'd nodded in return.
"Yes. They were just sex"
"And now?"
He'd leant forward and grasped both her hands in his "Now, it's different." He'd paused and looked into her eyes "You're different"
Busty couldn't have ignored the tingling of where he'd held her hands or the hope that had surged through her, but he had to think with her head. The man has had an affair with his brother's wife and betrayed Connor. Busty sighed, but no he hadn't betrayed Connor because John stopped himself from feeling anything. She shook her head; Connor would see it completely different though. As a man who felt many emotions and had no trouble showing them, he would certainly see John's actions as betrayal to him.
Suddenly she felt angry at Caroline. The woman was ruining everyone's lives just by being selfish and unfeeling. She wouldn't let Connor go because of something that had happened in the past, she'd slept with John because she didn't care who she hurt. But the fact that annoyed Busty the most was that no one could move on in their lives because Caroline was stopping everyone. Her own selfish reasons stopped Connor and Scarlet from being together and her selfish affair with John held Busty back from taking the leap.

She wasn't dumb; she knew John was at fault for embarking on the affair with Caroline, but she wanted to believe he was changing and the man who'd had countless affairs was a man she didn't know. She supposed the question she needed to ask herself was whether she wanted to risk her heart again and love a man who was trying to change into a better person. Busty had no doubt that if she entered a relationship with John that many things from his past would come back to haunt her.

She needed to find out if she was strong enough to cope with his past.

"So, where do you want to go to lunch?" Scarlet asked getting up and getting her coat.

Busty stood as well, even though she was still lost in her thoughts. "I don't know"

"Are you sure you don't want to tell me this secret? It seems to be on your mind constantly"

"I can't. But Scarlet, I do want to say that you're doing the right thing trusting Connor"

"Huh?"

"He says to you things aren't what they seem between him and Caroline and he's right. Caroline isn't in love with him anymore than he is with her"

"Why are you telling me this? How do you know?"

Busty swallowed. "Trust me. I just know ok? Now let's not talk about this anymore"

"No no no no" Scarlet said as she shook her finger at Busty "You are not giving me a little tip bit like that without an explanation. You know I'll be dying of curiosity now"

"Just, trust me Scarlet. Connor will come through for you"

She narrowed her eyes at Busty "Everyone asks me to trust them, but they don't tell me anything. You know my issues with trust"
"Yes I do. And you know mine, yet you're telling me to trust John"
Despite Scarlet's annoyance she smiled "Touché"

"Connor I've been meaning to tell you something" John began, clearing his throat. He looked down at his fingers and saw they were shaking. He dreaded this, he dreaded telling his brother something that would probably destroy whatever foundations they'd began building.
"Sounds serious" Connor answered from behind his desk. He was surprised when John had called him and asked if he could come down but was delighted to see his brother nevertheless.
"It is"
"Are you ok?"
"No. What about you?"
Connor laughed "John, cut to the chase. You look all nervous and fidgety and it makes me nervous, so just come out and say-"
"I've had an affair with Caroline" he blurted out stopping Connor in mid-sentence.
The two brothers stared at each other in silence. Connor's mouth was open and he looked completely shocked. John inwardly hit himself; *of course he looks shocked you've told him you've betrayed him with his own wife.*
"Connor" he began but stopped when Connor held his hand up. The quiet tension between the two was so prominent that John felt himself begin to sweat with nerves. Why couldn't Connor shout or throw things at

him? Why was his brother staring at him with disbelief shining in his eyes and hurt etched on his face?
"You've been sleeping with Caroline" Connor repeated quietly.
"Yes"
"Why?" he whispered
"Connor…I wish I could say I loved her or that I cared for her a great deal, but I have to be honest with you." John took a deep breath "Caroline was just another woman I ended up…using"
"You bastard" the insult was whispered so quietly that John almost didn't hear it.
"I know"
"Why her?"
"Con…" John shrugged, helplessness in his expression "I can't tell you why. I don't *know* why. I was a different man; I didn't feel anything, not guilt or remorse or…anything"
"And now you feel?"
"Yes. I feel things. I'm so sorry Connor; I don't know what to tell you"
Connor laughed spitefully "So now you've changed from being a lying son of a bitch, into a man who fees all type of emotions and wants to make amends?"
"Yes. I do, I want to start over and make amends"
Connor just shook his head disgust evident on his face.
"I've never done anything to you John, I've always tried to be a brother to you and you pushed me away"
"I was beaten Connor" John snapped his patience wearing thin "I was hit with Dad's belt time and time again, this scar" he pointed to his face "Is only one I got from him"

"Oh, poor Johnny boy was beaten so that excuses him from sleeping with my wife!" Connor shouted his anger flaring to life.
"No!" John yelled back "No" he said again this time more quietly. "It doesn't excuse anything but I'm trying to make you understand why I was who I was. I was brought up to feel nothing, to not showing anyone how I was feeling"
Connor sighed and held his head in his hands "Jesus John, you knew how I felt about Caroline and her…customers. You sat there while I told you how unhappy and empty I was and all along you were HAVING SEX WITH MY WIFE!"
John shot up from his chair and walked over to Connor. "Look, I get that you're angry but when you calm down you'll look at the situation and see it from my point of view"
"Get away from me John, just leave me alone."
"No, not until we have sorted this"
Connor looked at his brother and snarled at him "We'll never sort this out. Do you know how my life has been these past six years? Do you know how close I've come to grabbing a bottle of pills and ending it all?"
John shook his head "You'd never end your life"
"I was damned near close!" Connor sighed and braced his hands on the desk turning his head to look at John beside him. "How long have you been sleeping with her?"
"About a year"
"Did you like it?"
"Connor-"
"No. Tell me" Connor looked down at his clenched hands "I need to know"

"I did enjoy it. But she never used my name and I never called her by her name. It wasn't Caroline, your wife I was having sex with. It was…just a woman"

"But why did it have to be her?"

John held out his hands in frustration. "She came and propositioned me and-"

Connor looked up sharply "What?"

"She came and propositioned me one day and I just…I said yes. He was willing and I was….willing as well, I guess"

"She was the one who came to you first?" Connor repeated

"Yes"

Connor slowly sat down in his chair his eyes wide. "It's been going on for ages" he whispered

"What has?"

He laughed mockingly at himself "I've been such an idiot. She used me when we first met and when we married she was still using me."

"Using you?"

"Yes" Connor looked at his brother, wondering if he could ever get past this and if he and John could share a proper brotherly bond. He'd always be weary of his brother though, after this betrayal. But the fact that Caroline initiated it just proved to him how much he needed to be free of her.

"She's been married to me for a long time and yet she hasn't been faithful to me since we started going out. She holds the secret over my head telling me it would hurt me if I told anyone. How wrong she is"

John walked to the chair he was seated in before and looked at his brother. "Why don't you use this to you advantage?"

Connor looked confused "Use what?"

"My…um affair with Caroline. Say you found out about it and you're leaving. Then we'll do what we planned. If she starts threatening you about telling people you were the reason she lost her baby then I'll step in"
"Do you think it will work?"
John shrugged "Why don't we find out?"
"Now?"
"No time like the present, and you want to be with Scarlet don't you?"
"Yes. So much"
John stood and gestured to the door "Then let's go"
Connor stood as well, and grabbed his coat. As they walked to the door John put a hand on his arm. "Con, we'll be alright won't we?"
Connor looked at his brother and saw the sincerity of his gaze. He just didn't know if he could forgive him. "I don't know, John, let's get Caroline out of our lives first"
"Then we'll see?"
Connor nodded, looking at his brother in the eye. "Then we'll see." He repeated.

"You're what?" Caroline asked laughing at her husband.
Connor gritted his teeth "I'm leaving you"
She looked at Connor then looked at John and began to laugh again. "Come now Darling, we both know you can't leave me, so why do you keep torturing yourself?"
"I can leave you. I am."
She smiled icily at him "You're going to go to that slut aren't you?"

Connor clenched his fists "Scarlet is not a slut, Caroline. And that is rather hypocritical of you"
Her eyes narrowed but she gracefully sat down, her ankles locking together and her hands in her lap.
"You know I am not like that anymore"
Connor scoffed "What crap"
Caroline looked from Connor to John and their eyes met for a split second before he broke eye contact. *So he's told him,* she thought.
"If you're referring to my relationship with John that is because we're in love"
Now it was Connor's time to laugh. He laughed loudly, holding his stomach and throwing his head back. "Oh, Caroline" he said as he chuckled once more and wiped a tear from his eye "You never really changed from the naive girl you were when I first met you"
"And you never changed from the man desperate for love or affection" she snapped back. Connor's humour sobered up and he looked at her with hatred burning in his eyes.
"That's so wrong is it? To want love and affection from someone?"
"It's all fake. Love is fake, affection is fake. You have to look after yourself in this world"
"If you think love is fake why you do think yourself in love with John?"
Caroline looked at John, wishing he would meet her eyes. She knew that John would leave her one day but she never expected him and Connor to join forces against her.
"John and I share the type of love that does exist"
"And what type is that, Caroline?"
She raised her chin "Lust. Sex" she answered simply, looking at her husband.

Connor shook his head at his wife, hating her for sitting there so elegant as if nothing could hurt her. “That isn’t love”

“How would you know Connor? You haven’t experienced sex or lust for…” Caroline tapped her chin with her index finger “Six years”

Connor looked away towards John who had remained silent throughout his and Caroline’s conversation.

“Let’s get this done with” he said to John, who nodded back.

“What done with?” Caroline’s cool, icy voice asked.

Connor turned back to her “I told you. I’m leaving you. I’m going to be with Scarlet and I’m going to live the type of life I’ve craved since six years ago”

Caroline stood and walked calmly over to her husband “Connor, you know what is going to happen if you leave me”

He shook his head “There’s no point threatening me. I’m leaving you”

“Do you want everyone to know about what happened six years ago? Do you want to be questioned by the police?” she looked at John then back to Connor “Do you want people to find out that you’ve been lying to them all these years”

Connor swallowed “Caroline, Caroline” he chided “we both know if the secret got out it would hurt you more than me”

Her lips thinned into a tight line “Your career would be ruined”

He moved closer to her “You know I don’t give a damn about my career”

“How about everyone you represent? Their careers would be hurt by being associated to a man who has lied”

Connor cursed inwardly. He hadn't thought about his clients and what it could mean for them if he left Caroline. Damn! Just when he'd summoned enough courage to leave her, she gave him another reason why he couldn't. He was about to turn and walk away when he heard John's voice.

"His clients won't be hurt"

She looked at John and sauntered over to him leaving Connor watching them both. "How do you know" her voice dropped to a seductive whisper "Mr. Black?"

John smiled at her "Caroline, you should know me well enough by now to know that I have many associates." He looked at his brother his gaze kind when he said "And my associates would help Connor out with his clients"

Connor smiled back at John and an unspoken message went between them. Caroline watched the two brothers, starting to feel desperate. She couldn't lose both of them! Her whole life would change if she allowed them to get away with this. *Calm down*, she told *herself, now is not the time to lose control. Not in front of them.*

"Are you helping your brother now?" she asked

John's gaze hardened when he looked at her. "It's about time I started to"

Caroline smiled and shook her head, walking away from both brothers. They watched her as she settled in a chair.

"So, I take it you boys have agreed to help each other now." She clapped her hands quietly; mockingly at the two of them "It's about time. However I don't appreciate how you're both… ganging up on me" she clucked her tongue. "I suggest you both stop this nonsense and we can all go back to the way things were"

"Caroline" Connor said quietly "you don't understand. I'm leaving you, the secret be damned. John is leaving you; he has a new girlfriend now" at this news Caroline's head snapped around to John, her eyes wide with shock. Connor continued "And from today onwards you no longer have a hold on me. Tell everyone the secret if you want but as I said before, it will hurt you more than it will me."
"Why are you so…adamant about leaving now?" she demanded
Connor smiled "I have a reason to get out of this marriage. She has red hair and a bright smile"
Caroline scoffed at Connor's tone "Pathetic"
"It's not pathetic, Caroline" John said as he stepped towards her "it's called love. You believe what we shared was love, but it wasn't. It was never that"
Caroline bit her lip to stop from shouting at him. Why couldn't he see that they did share love, but their version of it? Caroline knew she and John were similar as they both didn't express their emotions, but it didn't mean they didn't feel anything. She looked at the man before her not recognising him. This was a man who wanted to feel and who wanted to share emotions. She didn't understand why he had changed to be like Connor.
"Believe what you want, John, but you think you have changed now, but you'll come back to me"
"No, I won't"
"Neither will I" Connor said, going to stand by his brother.
She looked at both men and smiled slowly. "You'll both regret it"
Connor shook his head "Why would I regret leaving the one person who has caused me so much misery?"

Caroline stood, facing Connor "People haven't seen the real you yet Connor Belle. When they do, they'll turn from you"

"No!" he shouted, taking a menacing step forward "I know who I am" he hissed at his wife's face "I know I'm a man who values people. I have morals and I have done my very best to stay with you and love you. But you wouldn't let me because you're a cold hearted woman." He sneered at her, look into her eyes "We could have had everything Caroline, but your selfishness and heartlessness ruined it"

"It isn't all my fault, Connor. You know about my past, I can't help the way I am!" she yelled at him, knowing she was beginning to crack but not being able to stop herself

"Yes, you could have!" he gestured to John "He's changing! He's changing into a better man and he has a dark past as well." Connor shook his head. "You use what happened to you as an excuse for being this cruel, evil woman. You'll live a lonely and miserable life now Caroline, you'll live what you made me live for six fucking years!"

He grabbed her by the shoulders and shook her "I loved you" he whispered roughly "And you threw it in my face. You rejected me and what I could offer you. Instead you were glad our child died, you were glad about that night six years ago when you-"

"Enough!" she shouted

Everyone was silent. Connor still had Caroline by the shoulders and he released her, stepping away and running a hand through his hair.

"I'm leaving now Caroline. I don't want to see you or talk to you. This part of my life is over."

"How do you know you will find happiness, Connor?" she whispered.
He closed his eyes, imaging Scarlet's smiling face and happy eyes looking at him. He opened his eyes again and looked at the woman who had tried and almost succeeded to ruin his life.
"I'll be happy" he said. He looked at his brother and jerked his head towards the door. They both walked towards it and were about to exit when they heard Caroline's voice behind them.
"As long as I am around the past will never leave you"
Connor turned his head and saw her standing in the doorway. Her words echoed in his ears and all he could do was turn away. He knew that even if he travelled across the world he wouldn't be able to escape because Caroline was right.
He would never be free of the past.

Chapter Ten

Scarlet sat on her sofa watching the television. She hadn't heard from Connor all day and refused to ring him. She wanted to give him some space. Although she did trust him, she wondered when they could be fully together. They stole a few hours here and there, but he always had to leave. Either because of Caroline, John or his work. Since the night of her party they had been trying to restrain themselves from continuing their sexual encounters; they'd both agreed it made it harder to stop before they went all the way. She felt like screaming! She just wanted him to take her hard up against the wall, on the bed, in the shower…the list went on and on. She supposed she should feel happy that he refused to consummate their relationship while he was still living with Caroline, but it didn't help the matter of her sexual frustration.

Argh! She had to stop her hands from wandering places, touching the place where she desperately craved Connor's touch. She had touched herself once, once when she was in bed, dreaming of him next to her. Even after bringing herself satisfaction, she hadn't felt fulfilled. Her touch was one thing but to feel Connor moving in and out of her, to feel his delicious weight on top of her….she couldn't wait! But she had to be patient. Connor was man who valued his morals and she couldn't ask him to do something that he didn't feel right about. All she knew was that he was a better person than she was. She got up, sick of sitting around and thinking about sex. Sex with Connor. Feeling Connor's muscled body, feeling his bare chest rubbing against her breasts….Argh! She stomped into the

kitchen and pulled out a piece of Dairy Milk chocolate and chewed angrily on it.
She decided her house was too quiet and needed something to take her mind off sex. She went back into her lounge, still munching the chocolate and put the CD player on. Marvin Gaye's voice came on, singing "*Let's get it on*" Scarlet closed her eyes and groaned thinking about the irony of that song coming on. Nevertheless the song came out of the speakers and the melody wrapped itself around Scarlet, and she found herself swaying and singing to it. "Trying hold back this feeling for so long…." She sang, putting another piece of chocolate to her mouth. "Let's get it on…" she twirled and stumbled a few paces, causing her to laugh at herself.
"That's so sexy" a voice said from the doorway. Scarlet shrieked and turned around to find Connor standing there, leaning against the doorframe, a predatory grin on his face.
"You scared me" she said, walking towards the CD player to turn it off
"No. Don't" he said, walking over to her and moving her hand out of the way so she couldn't turn off the music.
She laughed and looked at Connor but her laugh died down when she saw the stark hunger that flared to life in his eyes. They didn't speak, but they both knew that they were going to be together tonight. Now.
Scarlet wasn't sure who made the first move but she found herself in Connor's arms, his mouth firmly on hers and his hands gripping her tightly. Their kiss boarded on desperation and they grabbed each other roughly, the urge to feel skin on skin almost too much to bear. Scarlet yanked her mouth away from his to

undo the buttons on her shirt, Connor followed suit, fumbling with his buttons. In the end he yanked the shirt apart, the buttons flying everywhere. Scarlet looked at him in surprise then her gaze was riveted to his bare chest. Although not as muscular as most men she could see he had definite strength. His shoulders were broad, causing his chest to stand out and his nipples began to peak under her gaze. Scarlet licked her lips and wrenched her shirt of her slim shoulders. She ran her hands up and down his bare skin, savouring the feel of his warmth and softness. Connor reached around her and undid her bra, throwing it across the room. He cupped both breasts in his hands, loving how they filled his handful perfectly. His thumbs rubbed over her erect nipples and he watched the expressions of pleasure that were shown on her face. He bent his head and licked at one nipple, his thumb still teasing the other.

"Connor" she gasped. Connor continued his actions until he felt her pull his hair. He looked up and saw the impatience on her face. "Get your trousers off" she demanded, causing him to smile wolfishly. He didn't hesitate as he unzipped his trousers and pushed them down his strong legs, taking his boxers with them. He stepped out of them and kicked them away and then he stood there. Gloriously naked and for her eyes only. Scarlet stopped in the process of taking her trousers off to stare at him. He was….magnificent, she thought. A trail of hair led from his naval down to his erect cock and swirled around the base of it. She looked at it, thinking how big it was when it began to harden even more. Her gaze shot up to Connor's and he smiled at her.

"What do you expect when you look at me like that?" he took her in his arms and kissed her again, reigniting

the hot passion that had consumed them only seconds before. Their tongues battled, and Connor began fondling her breasts again. She moaned and pushed her trousers down, past her hips where they fell in a heap on the floor. She stepped out of them, kicking them away, leaving her standing in her silk black thong. Prince's song "Kiss" came on the stereo, causing Connor to break away from the kiss and laugh.
"I take it this is an album you made" he gasped
"Yes. I called it "Sexy Songs""
Connor grinned, his eyebrow rising "Well then, let's keep the theme going"
"Oh, yes"
He resumed kissing her, his hand slowly dipping past her breasts and down to her stomach until he came up against the underwear she wore. "This won't do" he whispered. He knelt down beside her and took her thong off slowly, leisurely at odds with the urgency in his gaze. He slid them past her smooth thighs and down over her legs. She stepped out of them, resting her arm on Connor's back for support. He flattened his hand as he trailed it up her leg, to her thigh, and then to the centre of her. She gasped and he looked up. "My beautiful Scarlet" he whispered, before his fingers parted her folds and he bent his head between her thighs. At her startled breath, he touched her clit with his tongue, slowly at first then increasing the rhythm. Scarlet moaned louder this time, pushing his head closer to her while grabbing at his hair.
"Connor….Oh Connor…..keep going….." she panted, nearly at the brink of climax. Suddenly, before she knew what had happened, Connor was standing in front of her and picking her up. She opened her legs and wrapped them around his waist. She was dimly aware

of once being in the position when they'd had clothes on and look forward to feeling the real thing. Connor poised himself at Scarlet's entrance, but before plunging inside he looked into her eyes. "Scarlet" he whispered. She could tell what he was saying, of what he was asking. If this was what she wanted.

She nodded, pulling his face closer to hers so that when she talked her lips brushed his "Connor, I've been waiting for you for so long" she whispered "I need you inside me right now. I need you to pound me hard and be with me"

At her words he groaned and kissed her. When he pushed his tongue in her mouth, he flexed his hips pushing himself into her. She cried out at the feeling, loving how he moved smoothly and easily.

"God, Scarlet, you're so tight…feels…so good" he panted, pushing himself in and out of her quickly, supporting her with his arms. He walked over to the sofa and, still joined, fell onto it. Connor rose on his arms, looking down at Scarlet's closed eyes and flushed cheeks. He gritted his teeth, trying to hold out until she found her pleasure, but God it felt fucking amazing! He plunged into her harder and harder, their skin slapping together and their moans growing louder and louder. Connor slowed his pace as he lifted one of her legs over his shoulder so he could go deeper. Scarlet whimpered at the new pressure and felt herself beginning to come apart.

"You're so wet, your pussy is just grabbing my cock so tightly," Connor moaned "God Scarlet" On his last word he reached down his thumb finding her most sensitive spot. He began to rub it like he had done with his tongue earlier. "Connor!" she shouted as her body began to spasm. She moaned loudly feeling the

delicious ripples skittle through her body. She was aware of Connor's hoarse shout and she felt him stiffened inside her as he came. He collapsed on top of her, his arms still holding most of his weight. Eventually their breathing slowed and he slid out of her and gathered her in his arms.
"That was….well…I can't describe it" She said, her hand weakly reaching up to touch his face. When she couldn't find it she let her arm fall away. "I'm tired" she whispered, snuggling closer to Connor.
"Hey, I'm the man. I'm supposed to be the one who goes to sleep afterwards"
"Well we can both go to sleep" she peered up at him under half closed eyes "Do you want to come to bed with me?" she asked coyly.
He smiled. "It's my dream" he said, kissing her gently on the nose. Connor stood, still naked and picked Scarlet up and carried upstairs to her bedroom. He laid her down gently then went to the bathroom to fetch a wet cloth. He cleaned the remains of their lovemaking and then settled next to her on the bed. He pulled the covers over both of them and held her close. Connor felt a sense of peace inside himself and he sighed contently and fell into a deep, happy sleep. Something he hadn't done for a while.

"You told her then?" Busty asked
John nodded "Yeah. Basically now Connor is free of her and hopefully so am I."
She sighed and smiled at him. "Hey, that's great news, I'm happy for you"
"For us" he corrected.
Her smile fell and she looked down at their clasped hands. "John…"

"No" he shook his head "Please don't tell me something I don't want to hear"
"I'm trying to be honest with you"
"I only want you to be honest with me if it's something I want to hear" he said with a small smile. She couldn't help but smile back. "It's difficult John. I mean Connor and Scarlet know each other a lot better than we know each other, so it makes sense for them to…take the next step and live happily ever after."
"We won't have sex until you're ready" he offered, inside thinking he was an idiot for suggesting something he probably couldn't keep. It wasn't his fault Busty was an unbelievably attractive woman.
"It's not just sex. It's the whole relationship thing. I was hurt so much and I don't know if I'm ready to give you my heart"
"We'll start small then" he suggested
"Small?"
"Sure. We'll date like you said the other night. We'll go out…to the cinema…and get some food. We'll just date"
"Will that be enough for you though?"
He swallowed "Well, I'll be honest. No it won't be enough for me. I want you Busty. I want you now. I'm a very impatient man as you know. But" he said at her sad expression "For you, I am willing to try and change that. So I'll be patient and I'll…woo you"
"John Belle wooing a woman?" she asked, giggling.
"I know, see what you've made me become?" he asked, smiling at her.
"Do you think it's finally finished with Caroline then?"
John shrugged "It is between me and her. As for Connor…I don't think he'll ever be fully free of her. Unless…."

"Unless what?"
He looked at Busty "Unless she died"
Confusion marred her face "Well, she's not going to die is she?"
He shook his head "No. Though it would make things a lot easier"
"John, don't speak like that"
He laughed "Come on Busty, you know I would never hurt another human being"
"How did Connor take it when you told him about your affair?" she asked, changing the subject. Talk about death made her uncomfortable, especially when it was about a woman whose death would benefit everyone.
John sighed "Not very well. But then what can I expect? The fact that Caroline has been screwing around on him since they met upset him more than the fact that she was with me. I think it made his decision up as well"
Busty chewed her nail "How do you mean?"
"Well, it was just the final straw I guess. He'd had enough and we went straight over to their house and told her"
"How do you think she took it?"
John looked at Busty and shook his head "You know what, I don't know. Caroline never let's anyone see what she doesn't want them to."
"You don't think she's…dangerous?"
"No, not physically dangerous." He smiled ruefully "Mentally she is"
"Well, I hope she leaves us alone now"
He smiled at her comment. "You mean there is an "us"?"
"Of course there is, but I just don't know how much of an "us" there is yet"

He grinned at her smugly "There's going to be a massive "us""'
She shook her head although she laughed. "We'll see"

The next morning Scarlet awoke in the arms of the man she loved. There was now no doubt about the fact that she loved Connor. Last night had just confirmed all her feelings. She remembered Connor's lovemaking and everything he had done to her and shivered with delight. She looked at his sleeping form, all peaceful and vulnerable. She decided it was time to pay back the favour he did for her last night. She ducked under the covers, moving slowly and quietly down his sleeping body, stopping when she got to his fully aroused cock. She took him in her hand and squeezed gently at first, then harder as she began to move up and down. He mumbled something in his sleep and jerked his hips, moving his cock in her hand. She listened to his even breathing, realising he was still asleep. She continued her hand movements until she decided to bend her head and lick the head of him lightly. His hips jerked again as if he was asking for more. She smiled and bent her head, taking him fully in her mouth and sucking on him gently yet firmly.
Connor was having the most erotic dream. Someone was licking and fondling him; he moaned urging the dream woman to continue. He heard a responsive moan and somewhere in his subconscious he thought that the moan sounded too real to be in his dream. He supposed he should open his eyes and see what was going on, but his dream felt so good. The woman was now fondling his balls, gently tugging on them while continuously sucking him. He suddenly opened his eyes looking around the room and noticing it wasn't his. Everything

came back to him in a flash. He was with Scarlet, this was her room, which meant she was under the sheet sucking his…..Ah! He sighed, it felt so good. He was nearly close to climaxing when he pulled her up by the arms and smiled at her "Hey you" he whispered before reaching down and opening her legs. He put his fingers inside her and was welcomed by a wet warmth. He groaned again, "Forgive for not giving you more foreplay" he said as he brought her up to straddle him. "Being with you is enough foreplay" she whispered, looking down at him. She rose up and then settled down, taking him inside her. She threw her head back and began to ride him. He reached up to cup her breast in his hand and let the other one hand fall down to where they were joined. He looked at her face as he found her clit and rubbed it like he had done the night before. She cried out and touched her own breasts as he continued touching her. She increased her rhythm going up and down on his hard cock, savouring the feeling of him sliding in and out of her. They climaxed together as he yelled out and his body stiffened, pushing upwards impaling his cock deep inside her as he came. Scarlet cried out and felt her body spasm as she leant down on top of Connor. The delicious currents continued to run through her body as she let her breathing slow.

"Now that was a nice way of saying morning" Connor said, stroking her hair

"Yes" she breathed "I certainly like it"

He kissed her on the side of the head then got up and went to the bathroom. When he returned he got back into bed and hugged her close.

"I can't believe we've finally don it" she murmured.

"I know. I feel so good to finally be with you in every way"
"Connor, I know you value your morals but I don't want you to feel ashamed about what we did last night"
"And this morning" he added
She smiled up at him "Yes. But I don't want you to feel bad…"
"Why would I feel bad?"
"Because ultimately you're still married"
He shook his head "I'm separated now"
It a few moments for His words to sink in but when they did Scarlet sat up and looked at him with disbelief.
"You told her?"
"Yes. I told her yesterday. John came with me"
"Why didn't you tell me?" she demanded, her hands settling on her hips. Connor looked at where her hands were, then at her hips, and then his gaze travelled up to her gorgeous breasts.
"Hello? My eyes are up here" she said. He smiled at her and rolled onto his back, his arms behind his head.
"You should take it as a compliment" he said with a wink. She smiled despite her frustration.
"Why didn't you tell me?"
"Because" he said as he pulled her back into his arms "we were busy doing other things. Then you wanted to go to sleep. So I'm telling you now"
"Well, you should have told me before" she grumbled, settling into his embrace
"What? I should have stopped touching your clit right before you climaxed and said "By the way I broke up with my wife…"" he snorted "That would have changed the mood dramatically"
She hit him playfully on the arm "I didn't mean like that. But tell me! What happened?"

"Ok, ok…" Connor explained exactly what had happened between him, Caroline and John, leaving no details out. When Scarlet asked how she took it, Connor answered the only way he could.
"I don't know. Caroline…doesn't give a lot away"
"So, you don't know if she was angry or not?"
"Well I think she was angry, but she didn't show it. She would never show any emotion that made other people believe she wasn't in control."
"Wow. So it's finally over" Scarlet said, smiling, thinking about all the happy days her and Connor had in the future.
"Um, Scarlet, I'm changing the subject here, but I need to know whether or not you're…on the pill?"
Scarlet stared dumbly at him for a second, then exclaimed "Oh!" she cleared her throat, feeling embarrassed for some reason "Yes I am. So no need to worry"
He looked relieved and she couldn't help but tease him a bit. "Would having a baby with me be so bad?"
The expression he gave her was a mixture of shock, disbelief and fear. She couldn't help but laugh at him.
"I'm teasing you my dearest Connor; I don't want a baby at the moment anyway" he nodded but still looked unsure "Come on I was joking" she said.
"Ok, but jeeze don't frighten me like that"
"Frighten? It was supposed to be a joke"
"I know but it seemed as if you wanted to get pregnant."
She frowned at him "Well I do. One day"
Connor nodded but didn't say anything. "Do you want a child?" she asked
He looked at her "Someday sure. But at the moment I just left Caroline. Let's get her out of our lives first"

"I wasn't suggesting…don't worry" they remained silent for a while, Connor idly playing with a strand of Scarlet's hair and Scarlet wondering why Connor stiffened up when she spoke of children. She understood that he had lost a baby when a burglar had broken into his house one night and that must have been devastating, but she thought that would have made him want one even more. She thought back to the story Busty had told a few months ago were a man had broken into the Belle's house and pushed Caroline down the stairs. That was the night were a big incident had happened, which caused all the secrets between Connor and Caroline now. Her eyes narrowed as her mind thought back to six years ago. Connor had always proclaimed that the secret between him and Caroline was something that couldn't be told to anyone and yet John knew. Why couldn't she know what it was now? After all the secret was bound to come out if he'd truly left her.

"Connor, what happened six years ago?" she felt his body stiffen and his hand stopped playing with her hair.

"Why do you ask?"

Scarlet leant up and looked at him "Well, you've left her now so there's no harm in telling me"

"But I doubt the secret will be known to everyone"

"I thought you always said that the reason you couldn't leave Caroline was because she threatened to tell this secret to everyone"

"Yes, she did threaten to do that"

"So, why wouldn't she tell everyone now?"

"I had John with me. He made it clear that she had nothing to gain if she told everyone what had happened. In fact we both made it clear that it would hurt her more than it would hurt me"

"Ok then. So why can't you tell me?"
Connor sat up and scooted to the edge of the bed. He scratched his chin and looked at Scarlet. "Well, there's no need to know it now is there?"
"I thought you wanted a proper relationship"
"I do" he said quickly
Scarlet wrapped the covers around her nudity and pushed her hair out of her face. "How can we have that if you still don't trust me enough to tell me this secret?"
"I do trust you" he reached for her hand but she snatched it away, her patience wearing thin.
"Connor" she sighed "Why can't you tell me?"
"It's not my secret to tell. It's Caroline's"
Her anger snapped "Oh, now you're protecting your wife?" she retorted sharply.
He frowned at her tone "No, I'm not protecting her, but it's…complicated Scarlet, it's not my business anymore. I said goodbye to all that yesterday. I want to start fresh"
"And we will. When you tell me the secret. You say it's not your business but it sure as hell was your business for six years!" she got up and held the sheet around her. "That secret was the reason as to why you led a miserable life and now you're saying to me "it's not my secret""
"Look, its complicated Scarlet. You don't know what happened or what you would be involved in if you knew. I want to keep you away form that. I want to keep you clean from my dirty past with Caroline"
When Scarlet remained silent he continued "I want a fresh start with you. I don't want to contaminate what we have with all the crap I've had to deal with"

"Connor, I understand what you're saying, but what if the secret does come out? What if everyone finds out? Do you really want me to find out from someone else?"
"No! No I don't." he rubbed his face "Look, if Caroline does for some reason tell people, I'll tell you straight away"
"This isn't exactly fair considering I told you everything about my past, even the dirty parts."
Connor sighed, looking at the woman he loved. Did he want to withhold this truth from her? Did he want this secret to come between them? She was right; she had told him everything about her, even all the bits she thought disgusting. He just didn't want to ruin what they had; he didn't like the idea of Caroline intruding on what they shared. But looking at Scarlet now, her eyes genuine and knowing she loved him, he knew he was going to tell her. He would have to put his trust in her like she did in him.
"Ok" he said standing up and taking her hand, leading her to where he sat "Ok I'll tell you"
"Really?"
"Yes. I'll trust you as you trusted me. I just hope you know what you're letting yourself in for"
She smiled at him "Connor, I'm with you no matter what happened in your past"
He swallowed and looked her in the eye, "It all began six years ago…."

Chapter Eleven.

Caroline sat in the dark holding the gun limply in her hand. She knew what she had to do now. After everything that had happened, after everything she had tried to keep hidden, it was all going to come out in the end.
Might as well go out with a bang.

John and Connor met at the door of his house, both looking surprised to see each other.
"What are you doing here?" Connor asked
John shrugged "Caroline called me and asked me to meet her. She sounded distressed." He frowned "I've never heard her sound like that and I was worried."
Connor nodded "She sounded the same to me"
"And you came?"
Connor looked at his brother "I thought I hated her. I truly thought I hated her, but even after everything she's done to me, I still can't hate her. Not when I loved her so much at one time"
John patted him on the shoulder "You're not programmed to hate, Con"
"What do you mean?"
John looked around them both "You're just not the type of guy to hate anyone. You've got too much goodness in you. I'm the type of man who can hate"
"I thought you said that you're changing"
John looked Connor in the eye, his expression serious "I'm trying to change the way I act and the things I do. I doubt I can ever change the person I am on the inside"
"There is goodness in you, John."
"Connor, I want you to know that I am deeply sorry for what happened between me and Caroline. I really want

you to understand that I didn't feel anything. I know I can't justify my actions but when I didn't feel anything, nothing I did was wrong in my eyes…do you see what I mean?"
Connor nodded slowly at his bother "I think I'm beginning to. I can't say for sure that I can ever fully understand, John. I'm not you, so I can't understand, but I'll try to"
John smiled and felt tears swell in his eyes. The first tears he had felt form since he was a young boy. "You have no idea how much that means to me" he said.
Connor pulled his brother into a hug and patted his back. "You're doing well, John" he whispered.
"Well, well, well, isn't this a touching scene."
Caroline's voice said from behind them. They pulled apart and stared at her "Sorry for interrupting, but we have some business to get down to" she turned and started walking into the house "Follow me, gentlemen"
They both followed her in the house unsure of what the night was to bring.

"So, I welcome you to my home" Caroline announced as she swept her arms wide gesturing the large lounge that they stood in.
"Caroline, what's this all about?" Connor asked.
She smiled at him "Tonight, one of our lives will end"
"What?" John and Connor asked in unison.
"Do you really need me to repeat it?" she looked at their blank faces "Fine, tonight one of us is going to die."
"Why will one of us die?" John asked.
"I don't know" she said looking around the room
"Because I feel like stopping one of you men from

leaving me. And the only way to do that is through death"
"Caroline" Connor said carefully "What would you gain from killing one of us?"
Caroline looked at him as if he was stupid. "Because if one of us dies here tonight, and by the way it won't be me, then they'll be another secret to bind us all together." She looked at both of them "A secret that would be impossible to get out of"
"Caroline, why would you want me or Connor to stay with you if you knew that we'd rather be with someone else?"
"It doesn't matter if you want to be with someone else. The fact is, you won't be. You'll be with me"
Connor shook his head "What's wrong with you Caroline? You're acting…"
"Crazy?" she supplied
"Well, no not crazy but…" his words trailed off as he looked to his brother for help.
"I'm not crazy Connor; I've just reached my limit. You both know what I've been put through in my life and you both have accused me of being too cold and unfeeling, well I've had to be!" she shouted "I've never been given the chance to feel so why should I allow you two to *feel?* Why should you be happy?"
"Caroline, if you want to change the way you are, there's always time to…"
"No Connor! Don't you get it? I don't see why I should change; I believe everything I've done to you is what you have deserved. I feel no guilt or remorse for what I've done; I believe I am right in the way I've acted. Quite frankly, I haven't had any other choice."
"Then why do you want to kill one of us?" John demanded

Caroline huffed and rolled her eyes. “You two are so thick! I want to kill one of you so then I’ll have control again…it’s what I did last time and I gain control of Connor…” her words were mumbled as she talked to herself. Connor and John made eye contact, both knowing they had to get out of this house. Caroline looked as if she had reached breaking point and they both knew that they were stepping in dangerous territory. Connor moved slightly towards the hallway when he heard a gun shot. His head whipped around to see Caroline holding the gun up towards the ceiling. His eyes followed the smoking bullet hole that was now pierced there.

“Caroline…” he started, too shocked to finish his sentence.

She laughed at their shocked expressions “Now do you believe how serious I am? I have the gun which means I have the power.”

“Caroline, you don’t want to hurt me or John, you don’t like hurting people”

“I do!”

“No you don’t. What you did six years ago was a necessity; if you hadn’t done it he would have killed you”

She shook her head her hands trembling as she held the gun pointing between John and Connor. “I enjoyed it though. I felt powerful”

Connor remained silent, thinking back to six years ago when he arrived at his house after Caroline’s call. He remembered how she had seemed calm, even relaxed. She had told him what had happened and what they had to tell the police. She had then calmly explained about her past and what she had been doing behind Connor’s back. He looked at her now, realising now how much

that night had changed her. Connor knew that on that night six years ago, Caroline had snapped and the woman she was today was the result. The problem that he and John faced now though, was that he wasn't sure which woman he was talking with.
"Susie?" he asked quietly.
Caroline's head snapped up and looked at Connor.
"Why are you calling me that?"
"Because that was your name, Caroline"
"No, Susie died a long time ago"
"But she seems to be alive Caroline. She's alive and talking with us now"
Caroline put her hands over her ears "No, don't confuse me"
John stepped forward, catching on to what his brother was trying to do.
"It's ok Susie, no one blames you for what you did all those years ago." He said
Caroline looked at John "You weren't there"
"No, but Connor told me what you did and why you did it. You had no choice"
"You don't understand!" she shouted "I was glad to see his blood on her hands. I was glad because I vowed to myself that I would see his blood instead of mine. And I did and it felt so good"
"Susie…"
"No! I am not her, I am not that weak, pathetic woman who allowed Toby to beat her, I am the powerful woman who killed him"
"Susie…"
Caroline held her hands over her ears to stop from hearing that name. Once again she was thrown back into the past, to six years ago, where she had changed

to such a degree she didn't know who she was anymore.

Susie

Red faced, eyes blurred, cheeks flaming, ears ringing, she crawled along the new cream carpet, digging and clawing her fingers into it, trying to muster the strength to get away. Get away from this place. "Get away from him." she muttered quietly to herself.

The sky had turned dark, and the small, modest house shone underneath the moonlight. The old, oak rocking chair sat silently in the corner, as she pulled herself up using the wooden banister at the top of the stairs. She looked around herself, noticing her Picasso print hanging loosely on one corner, against the newly painted white walls.

Every thing went silent. Her crying had stopped along time ago, his mocking, teasing voice had been muted, and all that could be heard, was a deadly silence.

Her hands trembled violently as she looked at the blurry walls in front of her, trying to clear her mind and think about her next move.

His veins were pumping with the whisky he had guzzled only hours before. A nervous gasp stuck in her throat as she heard movement on the stairs below her. Still trembling and shaking, she peered over the top, looking down into the narrow gap of darkness, like a pathway leading to her endless torment. Her freedom was away, away from the monster with whom she was joined in holy matrimony.

"Susssie" the patronising sing song voice came from below the stairs.

She stiffened, not daring herself to make a move or reply. She knew if she did, then he would have her. Forever. Until the end of time.

Susie looked at the stairs leading downwards, she felt herself stiffen as her spine shivered with fear. She felt like a small prey running away from the predator. She could almost see the plan he had set out for her, to chase her, watch her squirm, then just as she was at breaking point, move in for the kill, and so far, Susie had allowed it to happen.

Later, she sat hard against the wall, trembling fiercely, as his eyes stared back at her. Wide, open, never wavering from her own. They didn't blink, they didn't move, just stared back at Susie. She thought back to the day they married; it had never been anything other than an arrangement, she had been forced to marry him, but she had hoped it could turn into something more.
And now he was dead.
Susie blinked. Then looked at her hand, clenching it tightly, and then releasing it.
She studied her fingers, shaking in disbelief at what she'd done. The word echoed in her brain.
She glanced back to Toby, laying there on then kitchen floor, and once again, those open eyes stared back at her. Still mocking her, still laughing at her.
Susie stood up on shaky legs, and steadied herself by holding onto the table. Her breath caught in her throat as those cold blue eyes stared at her, before she turned her back and waked away.
When she walked into the lounge she looked out of the windows, and saw it was snowing like confetti on the devils parade. She sat down silently. She placed her hands in her lap, neatly crossed over one another. The moonlight poured into the darkened room and shone upon her pale face as a small smile rose on her face. Her eyes strayed over to the bottom of the stairs, where she could see a puddle of Jack Daniel's whisky, as it

seeped through the cream carpet, staining it, leaving a painful reminder of his presence.
Suddenly a flare of fury rose within her as she got up and marched towards the stain. Staring down at it, she could still see the blue mocking eyes staring back at her, the same eyes that had watched her beg for mercy when in the past he had threatened to beat her.
She went into the kitchen, past his motionless body, and picked up a tea towel.
As she was scrubbing the stain, all anger vanished, and her eyes started to flood with salty tears of pain. Huge, racking sobs shook her whole body, and as her head fell into her hands and she fell to her side, crying desperately.
Her mind showed her what happened, over and over again. His laughter echoing in her ears and his harsh voice telling her she was nothing. His arm raising for another violent attack on her, and then she, suddenly, looking up into his eyes, and watching how they had betrayed the fear he felt for himself.
Another sob escaped her, as she lay on the floor. All that could be heard from outside the cottage, was distressed animals screaming like desperate pleas for help, and the clock, ticking slowly, signifying each painful second that passed by.
The sound when she stuck him down, vibrated in her ears, she didn't want to think about the deafening, haunting reverberation that had echoed throughout the house. She didn't want to think at all. She sat up and looked around herself. Her lips rose in a tiny, self-mocking smile. She then stood up on unsteady legs, and wiped her face clean of tears.
As she walked into the kitchen, she looked at the body still laying where it had been earlier, having not moved

an inch. Its motionless limbs were sprawled across the white tiled floor, one arm flung carelessly towards the dented frying pan, as the blood dripped slowly, almost teasingly, from his head.
Her eyes focused on the crimson liquid which had settled on the floor. She saw the path which it had run, in and out of the tiles, around the tiles, onto the tiles, drowning them until no white could be seen, like the devil claiming Susie's soul and all the good she once had inside her. Her eyes focused out of the window and she looked at the stars in the sky and the moon shining brightly. Her hand clench and un-clenched as she thought of what she could do. The dark shadow, that had haunted her since she married him, ceased to exist now, but the burden of knowing how it had been lifted away from her shoulders, was enough for anyone to take. She knew who would help her, and she picked up the telephone and pushed the numbers slowly. What if no one helped her?

Connor was working when he got the panicked call from Susie.
"Someone…broke into the house" she said, her voice cracking.
"Oh my God, are you ok? Is the baby ok?"
"I don't know Connor, I'm bleeding and I…I feel so scared. Will you come home?"
"Of course, give me fifteen minutes and I'll be with you" he put the phone down, shut his laptop up and rushed out to the elevator. He couldn't believe someone had broken into their house! Susie had said she'd been bleeding. Oh God, he thought, his worry etched on his face, he hoped she wasn't experiencing a miscarriage. They hadn't been married long but he loved Susie so

much and would do anything for her. They had met in a coffee shop where he had tried to charm her. At first she had been unresponsive and unfriendly, but he had charmed her out of her bad mood. They had had a whirlwind relationship, and he had asked her to move in and marry him after only three months of knowing her. She had gotten pregnant; something he was thrilled about. Susie had remained clam but he knew she was excited as well. Connor could burst with happiness, being with Susie made him complete. He only hoped she was ok.

When he arrived home he saw that no lights were on. He called out Susie's name but no one answered. He walked through the house looking for her. Then he came across the burglar's dead body. At first Connor though he must be imagining what he was seeing but when he blinked his eyes a few times and the body stayed were it was, he realized that a dead man was on his kitchen floor. "Susie!" he bellowed.
"He was going to attack me" a quiet voice said from behind him.
"Susie" he whispered and rushed to her side, pulling her into his arms. "Are you ok?" he ran his hands over her body checking for cuts or bruises.
"I'm fine. I killed him" she said quietly
"Yes…Oh God you killed him?" he looked back to the man and swallowed his panic rising. "Look, don't worry; you won't be in trouble with the police or anything. You had a right to defend yourself"
"I enjoyed it"
Connor snapped his head back around to Susie.
"What?"

She looked at him, her eyes flat and lifeless. Connor felt a shiver go through him at her expressionless face, worried at what effect this will have on her.

"There are things you need to know Connor, but I need your promise that you won't ever tell anyone what happened here. I need you to promise me that whatever happens we will continue our marriage."

Connor looked at her, confusion evident on his face "Of course we will. I love you"

She shook her head "You don't"

"Susie, why are you acting like this? Why are you being so…cold?"

She slowly looked at him, her face still neutral. "Cold? I'm not being cold, I'm being realistic."

"Is the baby ok?" he asked suddenly

She shook her head "No, I lost the baby Connor"

Connor felt the floor go out from under his feet. He stumbled against the kitchen door, holding it for support. Pain burst within his chest and hopelessness took hold of him.

"God…I can't believe it. How did…?"

"He pushed me down the stairs"

A strangled moan caught in his throat as he imagined his Susie getting pushed down the stairs and their baby bleeding out of her. He looked towards the man lying on the floor dead and felt glad that he had died.

"Susie, are you ok? Does it hurt? Do you want me to take to you the hospital?"

"No, Connor. Now isn't the time for that. I need to tell you things about my past"

He took her hand and led her to the lounge where he sat her down. "What things, baby?"

Susie closed her eyes, knowing this was the only way she could keep Connor in control for the rest of their lives. She wouldn't allow herself to be this woman anymore who pleased men and did what was told of her. She wouldn't be pathetic. When she had raised the frying pan, a powerful force had surged through her, and as she brought the frying pain down on Toby's head she had enjoyed the power and control she'd felt. Finally, for a second she'd had control over Toby and his life. She was the predator and he, finally was the prey.

She had enjoyed killing him. Now she felt a shift in her body as if she was currently changing who she was. She only felt a pleasant numbness and a sense of clarity. She needed to get Connor under her thumb; she needed to control him so she would never be at the mercy of anyone else. She never once considered what impact her decision that night would have on hers and Connor's life; she simply didn't care enough to think about anyone else apart from her need to be in control of her life.

And so, Caroline was born.

Chapter Twelve

John and Connor looked at the gun in Caroline's hand and felt fear. John let it in; he let himself feel the fear and knew he had to do something.
Caroline had held her hands over her ears for a few minutes now, muttering something to herself. He would have made a move to safety if her eyes hadn't been constantly on him and Connor. She was wide-eyed, covering her ears and shaking her head back and forth. To John, she looked like a crazy person.
"Caroline…" Connor said, now aware that calling her Susie didn't help matters. She stopped shaking her head and looked at him.
"Your secret won't go any further"
"You left me. Everyone will know now"
"No they won't" he insisted
"Crap!" she shouted spreading her arms wide, the gun hanging loosely from her fingers. "Everyone will know I killed my first husband and that I committed bigamy"
"Caroline, I made a promise to you that night remember?" Connor said gently, slowly making a step towards her "I promised you I wouldn't tell anyone"
"You also promised you would stay with me. But I've failed to control you."
"Ok, I'll make you another promise now." He took a breath "I promise I won't tell anyone about what happened. Even if I'm not with you, your secret will stay with me until the day I die" he looked earnestly into her eyes, trying to get her to connect to him. Even though she had been the reason for his misery, he didn't like seeing her like this.

She looked at Connor for a full minute and silence settled in the room. Connor thought he was getting through to her, but then she shook her head.
"No. You won't be here so I won't have control over you"
"Why do you need control so much? Can't you just trust me?"
She laughed hysterically "Trust you? No. Trust isn't enough; the only thing that works is if someone has control." She raised the gun and pointed it at Connor
"Ok ok," he said, his panic obvious in his voice "I'll stay with you, I'll stay with you and you can control me" he pleaded
She shook her head, her expression sad. "No, Connor, I know you won't. You promised you'd stay with me and you broke that promise. Goodbye" she whispered
She squeezed her finger on the trigger, but before she could pull it John ran into her, intending to push her arm out of Connor's direction. As he did, a shot rang out.
She screamed and clawed at his face, causing him to jump back. He looked at the crazed look in her eyes and knew he was in trouble if he didn't get that gun from her hand. He charged again, grabbing her hand and squeezing it until she dropped the gun. She punched him in the side of the head, pushing him away as she crawled along the carpet for the gun. She grabbed it, turned and aimed at John.
"No!"
A bullet left the gun in that instant. All that was left was silence.

Epilogue

One year later

Conner held the baby high in his arms making funny faces at the little boy. He smiled when the baby looked at him blankly and burped. He brought the child back down and settled him on his knee, patting his back.
Scarlet came into the room and smiled warmly at the sight of Conner and his nephew. She patted her increasing stomach and sighed contently; she had four more months to go and couldn't wait to give birth to Conner's child.
"Is he hungry?" she asked, bringing in Vincent's warmed milk.
"I'm not sure, he's just been burping at me" Conner replied looking at his wife.
Scarlet and Conner had married four months previously in a small ceremony. They both had discussed how they hadn't wanted to press involved so they did it quietly with only family and close friends as witnesses.
The press had been unkind to Conner and the Belle family in the past year, since the death of his wife.
Connor still had nightmares about that night and sometimes woke up screaming at Caroline to put the gun down. But in his nightmares she never listened to him, she always aimed it at John, waited for three long, agonizing seconds before she turned the gun on herself and shot. He sometimes shouted more than "No!" he sometimes ran towards her and nearly reached her in time, but she always died. He still saw her body slump forward, the gun leaving her hand with a clatter. The blood….oh he still saw the puddle of blood forming beneath her and he still heard himself out shout….

He sometimes confided in John that he felt as if he should have done more. That perhaps if he had gotten up quicker after being pushed out of the way…perhaps he could have reached Caroline and John before she got the gun… John always reassured him that he couldn't have done anything to prevent the outcome of that day. In a matter of seconds, Caroline took her own life and had died.

Sometimes, Connor still couldn't believe that she was gone and that she never coming back. He would be a liar if he didn't admit that sometimes he felt relieved that she was gone and that the hold she had over him was lifted. When he had first admitted this to Scarlet he had cried, scared he would disgust her with such evil thoughts. But she had held him close and told him she understood him. Even though Caroline would never know it, Connor vowed to himself that no one would discover the secret she had gone to such lengths to keep hidden. When he had told Scarlet his decision concerning the secret that had trapped him in his marriage with Caroline, she hadn't understood at first. She had gotten angry at him, yelling that it would be easier for everyone else to know. At the time of their argument, the police had still been investigating into the circumstances of Caroline's death, as they had believed there was more to it than a simple suicide. Scarlet had been scared that Connor would be charged with murder.

"I won't be!" he had yelled frustratingly "John was there the whole time, he is my alibi"

Scarlet had scoffed, her face a mask of anger "Oh sure, the police will believe your *brother*. You know they don't expect him to protect you as your *family*" she'd said sarcastically.

Connor had looked at her with a bleakness that still haunted Scarlet to this day
"What do you want me to do then, huh? Come on, tell me…I don't know what to do" his voice had cracked and he'd held his head in his hands as tears fell from his eyes to his cheeks. Scarlet had wanted to comfort him, to hold him close to her, but she didn't understand his need to keep on protecting Caroline and her damned secret.
"Tell them everything. Tell them that Caroline killed her husband in self-defense. Tell them Caroline was a bigamist and that you believed Toby was a burglar instead of her husband until recently"
Connor had lifted his head, the lines of his tears shining in the light of Scarlet's house.
"Then they'll investigate into that case." He wiped away his tears angrily. "And then it will be brought back into the press, it won't ever end." He'd looked at the woman he'd loved, willing her to understand his decision "Caroline and her secret will keep living. The more I speak about it, the more it lives. Do you not get that?!" he'd yelled, anger obvious in his dark expression. "Everyone will know that Caroline was a woman who had serious mental health problems. And then her history as Susie will come out and then everything she tired to do to keep it hidden will be for nothing." Connor had shook his eyes, his eyes still locked with Scarlet's "Do you want me to make her life worthless by telling people her secret? I can't and I won't. I won't fail her this time"
The silence following Connor's statement has been long and deafening.

"You still love her" Scarlet had stated flatly, her eyes lowering from Connors. She'd heard him sigh and his footsteps as he'd moved and stood before her.
"Scarlet, I don't love Caroline. I haven't for a long while. But if you're asking me to let everyone know what Caroline tried so hard to keep hidden, then you don't know me very well." He had taken her hands in his, their eyes locked together. "I feel as if I failed her, she kept going on about how I broke my promise to stay with her. And I did break my promise. It eats me up inside every time I hear her voice accusing me of letting her down." Connor had taken a shaky breath "I know that she had become so wrapped up in herself that she gave me no option but to leave her, but I never would have guessed what the outcome would bring"
"Connor, you were so unhappy and Caroline gave everybody the impression that she was…unshakeable. How were you to know that she would lose it? You're just a human, you make mistakes and you listen to me when I tell you that what happened to Caroline was not your fault. It wasn't your fault anymore than it was my fault"
Connor had looked at her tenderly, stroking her face with his finger "I still feel so…responsible though"
"It is only natural. You're a good man, Connor Belle and I know you wouldn't tell anyone what Caroline died trying to protect"
They had held each other through the night, discussing the guilt Connor felt and how he could make it better. They had both agreed not to tell anyone Caroline's secret in the end and had let the police carry on in their investigation unaware of the tragedy that had taken place six years previously. In the end the police couldn't find anymore evidence to suggest that it was

anything more than a suicide and had closed the case, labeling it a "Suicide" Connor had laughed humorlessly when he heard what they had called Caroline's case. He'd mused loudly by himself "As if it were that simple"

Connor hadn't seen John for a while in the months following Caroline's death. They had both agreed to have their space and to come to terms with what happened that night on their own. John, who had expected to deal with the whole ordeal on his own, was incredibly grateful when Busty had turned up at his door, demanding that he let her in.

He had protested that he could deal with it on his own but Busty had refused to leave until he'd talked about it. To his surprise, he found himself spilling all his emotions to her, savoring the fell of her holding him while he tired to explain the guilt he felt whenever he saw Caroline.

"She said she loved me" he'd admitted quietly.

"Perhaps she did" Busty had replied, touching his hand with hers.

"I didn't treat her very well though. Even throughout our affair I never felt anything for her, other than lust"

Busty had winced at the reminder of John's relationship with Caroline, but had nevertheless helped him talk through his emotions concerning their affair.

"You were that person, John. But now you're not, now you're the type of person who feels things and who doesn't use women."

He'd looked at her, his eyes shining brightly "But it's too late for Caroline"

Busty had swallowed and tried again to talk to him. She'd found it hard to talk to John about Caroline as she still felt a certain amount of jealousy and she was

ashamed of feeling it, considering everything Caroline and John had been through in their lives.
Suddenly an idea had popped into her head and she'd tried another strategy to get through to John "Why don't you use what Caroline taught you, John?"
"How do you mean?" he'd asked through confused eyes
"You discovered with her that you wanted to feel more for a woman. That you wanted to have more than just a sexual relationship with women didn't you?" at John's nod, she had carried on "Well, why don't you feel grateful to her for showing you what you didn't want? Learn by her mistakes and make your life better"
John had thought about it for a long while after Busty had suggested another way to view the situation. Slowly he had begun to take her advice and realize that he didn't want to have anymore regrets in his life. The day he decided to make each day count was the day he and Busty first made love. They began a new life together and in turn created a new life.
Connor looked at Scarlet, sitting on the edge of the sofa, making faces at Vincent, and smiled "I love you, you know?" he said.
She patted her growing stomach "You better! Because we've got a little girl on the way" he stared at her stomach in awe, amazed that his little baby girl was growing inside there. He could imagine a little baby girl with red hair and mischievous eyes. She would have Scarlet's dazzling smile and beautiful face. At first he'd had mixed feelings about Scarlet's pregnancy so soon after Caroline's demise, and had worried how the press would turn it into something dirty. But the day they both went to her first scan, and when he saw the tiny little peanut shape that was to be his baby, he had

forgotten all his worries and had felt an incredible feeling of joy. He'd grabbed Scarlet's hand in a tight grip and whispered, while still looking at the picture on the screen, "That's our baby"

Remembering that day caused Connor to take Scarlet's hand and kissed it, looking up at her with love shining in his eyes. "I'm so lucky to have you"

"I'm lucky to have you to Mr. Belle. I love you" she said simply. They smiled brightly at each other. Having overcome so much in the last year, their love was stronger than ever and they both knew that the birth of their baby girl would bring them even closer together.

The doorbell rang and Scarlet went to answer it. Conner lifted Vincent up again and smiled at him.

"Careful brother, don't want to hurt my son now do you?"

He laughed at John "You're so over-protective of this boy. You need to let him be a man"

"He's a baby!" Busty exclaimed walking over to her son. She had missed him so much!

She lifted him up, cradling his head to her chest, inhaling the unique scent of her baby son. She winked at John and said, "Never again am I letting you two and John convince me to leave Vincent"

"You needed some time away from him" John explained as he came up and stood beside Busty, bending to kiss her cheek.

"No I don't. I'm going to smother him so much, he'll become a recluse. Then he'll never leave me" she said with a grin.

John rolled his eyes "You say I'm over-protective, I'm nothing compared to her"

"Oi! Cheeky man" she said brushing a kiss to Vincent's head. She smiled at her husband and thought back to

the past year. Since Caroline's suicide, she and John had hardly spent a day apart. He showed her a vulnerability that was so intense; Busty had given herself completely to John. When they had found out she was pregnant, John had been so shocked that she still laughed when she recalled his dazed expression.
"A baby?" he'd repeated dumbly
"Yes, a baby!"
"You mean….a baby?"
"Jeeze John, yes a baby!" she exclaimed jumping up. John had sat still for another ten seconds before he'd jumped and swung her around in delight, shouting that he was to become a father.
Looking at her husband now she realized how far they had come since the night where they'd first met and although it hadn't been easy, it had been worth every minute of the anguish and pain the last year had caused them both.
He kissed her on the lips now and pinched her cheek. "Right, we best be off. Thanks Con," he looked at Scarlet "Scar. Come on my gorgeous wife, let's hit the road"
The women walked out first, chatting and making a fuss of Vincent. Conner and John followed at a slower pace.
"You ok?" Conner asked
"Sure. What about you?"
"I still have the nightmares" he admitted.
John stopped and looked Conner in the eye. Ever since that night, he and Connor had spent a lot of time apart and had only met up again eight months ago when Busty and Scarlet had demanded it. What their wives didn't understand though, John had thought at the time, was that he and Connor weren't angry at each other;

being apart and on their own was how they dealt with it. It was a strange feeling having a wife which meant John wasn't on his own anymore. He still pinched himself everyday to make sure he wasn't dreaming the joy he felt when he was with Busty and his son. He looked at his brother now and wondered at how far they both had come since that night with Caroline. They both had what they wanted in life one of which was a relationship with each other. John was certain Connor had forgiven him for having an affair with Caroline, although they had never spoken of it. Perhaps they would speak of it in the future, but John was content with leaving that matter to rest for the time being.

"I have nightmares as well Con, I think we always will. But…we need to look around at what we gained from that horrible day."

Conner nodded "I know. I know there wasn't any…other way that day could have ended, but I still feel…guilty."

John smiled at his brother "Of course you do. That's who you are." He looked at Busty and the back at Conner. "Remember our discussion about hate?" at Conner's nod John continued "Well, just like you're not the type of man to feel hate, you are the type of man to feel guilt. Especially for something you had no control over" John looked at his brother intently, willing him to take heed of his words. He squeezed his arm and began to walk towards Busty.

"Do you feel guilt?" Conner asked. John stopped walking and turned back to face his brother. His expression was somber, but his eyes were clear as they looked at each other.

"Everyday. But" he walked back to his brother and grasped his arm "I comfort myself with the fact that I

won't make the same mistakes as she did" He recalled how Busty had suggested that and hoped Connor would see the wisdom of her words.
Connor nodded at his brother, his expression thoughtful "I suppose you're right. I mean, look at us" they both looked towards their wives, who were arguing over what hat Vincent should wear "We have wives and children. We're not alone" Connor said simply, his gaze returning to his brother.
John nodded, a small smile appearing on his face "We aren't" he agreed. He squeezed Connor's arm again and walked towards Busty and his son. He looked at them and knew he would go to the end of the earth to make either of them happy, just to repay them for the happiness they gave him. Finally, he thought as he kissed Busty on the cheek and took Vincent into his arms, cradling him close, finally I have a life worth living.
Conner watched his brother walk away and put his arm around Scarlet as she joined him. He kissed her cheek and led her back into their warm house. John's words echoed in his ears and he knew his brother was right. He didn't want to waste his life making the same mistakes as Caroline did. He could finally celebrate the love he felt for Scarlet and his unborn daughter, knowing there was nothing that could stop him from doing so.
"Everything turned out ok, didn't it?" she asked him, looking up into his eyes.
"Yeah." He smiled tenderly down into her upturned face "Everything turned out perfectly" he said with a soft kiss against her lips. When he pulled back he looked at her, amazed at how she after everything that

had happened to them in the past year, their relationship was incredibly strong.

“I’m going to tell you how much I love you everyday” he vowed “and I’ll make sure you know how special and cherished you are to me.” He kissed her again, placing a hand on her swelling stomach “I won’t let any of you down”

And he didn’t.

www.ingramcontent.com/pod-product-compliance
Lightning Source LLC
Chambersburg PA
CBHW030925090426
42737CB00007B/327

* 9 7 8 1 8 4 6 9 3 0 6 8 3 *